*Basque Diaspora and Migration Series*
*No. 13*

# At Midnight

Javier Arzuaga

*With an introduction by* Angel Katarain

*Translated by* Cameron J. Watson

Center for Basque Studies
University of Nevada, Reno

*This book was published with the generous financial assistance of the Basque government.*

Basque Diaspora and Migration Series
No. 13
Series editor: Xabier Irujo


Originally published as *A la medianoche* in 2012 by Semillas en el Tiempo, Ordizia, Gipuzkoa
Book design by Dan Montero

Library of Congress Cataloging-in-Publication Data forthcoming

# Contents

# Introduction

Javier Arzuaga (1928–2017) was raised in the world of Spanish Catholic Francoism of the post–Civil War Basque Country. A son of Oñati, at scarcely ten years of age he was placed in the Seminary of Arantzazu by his family. When he was twenty-three he was ordained as a Franciscan priest and assigned to Cuba, the Caribbean island that was under the Franciscan missionary Province of Cantabria (directed from the Order's Iberian headquarters at the Monastery of Arantzazu). After serving as a professor at the seminary of Santiago de las Vegas, in 1956 Father Arzuaga was named the parish priest of Casa Blanca, located in Havana's harbor district adjacent to the fortress of La Cabaña.

During the final years of Fulgencio Batista's reign, Javier attempted to minister to the prisoners in the fortress. "We have no prisoners here," he was told by the commander, but, as chaplain, he was allowed to say mass for the mothers and wives of the soldiers. On January 6, 1959, after Castro's revolutionary forces entered the capital, the previous commander of La Cabaña was replaced by Ernesto Che Guevara. In their first encounter, after exchanging comments about the significance of their respective Basque surnames, Javier asked Che for permission to continue saying Sunday mass in the prison and to visit the prisoners as well. Che refused the first request. There would be no masses, catechisms or rosaries, nor Christians, Muslims, or Buddhists for his soldiers. On the other hand, Father Arzuaga could provide spiritual consolation to those prisoners facing trial. "You can visit them as many times as you like, at any hour and for as long as you want," were the words of Che. He also told Arzuaga to buckle up since he was going to have a lot of work along these lines. In short, there would be many prisoners.

And it was thus that Father Arzuaga began his descent into hell. One of the first measures of the new regime was to establish tribunals of justice to try alleged collaborators of the deposed dictatorship. Many of the fat cats had fled the country along with Batista, but many others remained trapped on the island. The detainees in Havana were imprisoned in the fortification of La Cabaña. According to Arzuaga, if there were two hundred bunks in the facility it soon housed more than eight hundred prisoners. And then began the trials—surrounded by an atmosphere of both disquiet and euphoria.

Those condemned to face the firing squad were transferred to a section of the prison known as the "*galera de la muerte*," the "Gallery of Death."

Javier was present at each of the fifty-five executions carried out between February and May of 1959. His book is the exceptional account of one who narrates what he experienced, without exaggeration and dispassionately, yet from the "darkness of his personal midnight." It was his destiny to not simply witness the events as a spectator, but rather as the pathetic consoler of the hopeless condemned men. "It is not easy to talk to a man with a death sentence," Javier used to say—and he had to speak with fifty-five. Whenever he brought this up his voice became distorted, and he struggled for the words that often seemed inadequate to him.

On the other side was Che, a man totally committed to the revolutionary war and now charged with exacting justice for Batista's repressors. As late as 1964, Che would tell the United Nations: "We have executed, we execute and we will continue executing for as long as it remains necessary. Our struggle is to the death." In La Cabaña he advised the mother of a condemned prisoner, "Madam, I recommend that he speak with Father Arzuaga, who, they say, is a master at consoling and raising spirits." Javier was desolate from the very first execution; nevertheless, he carried out his assigned duty with such zeal that Che ordered that no one should be shot unless the priest was present.

The anti-Castro propaganda claims that hundreds, even thousands, of persons were executed at La Cabaña during this time; albeit Arzuaga places the number between February and May of 1959 at a more modest fifty-five. However, while he reduces the absolute number in quantitative terms, he does so with such empathy and intensity as to situate the subject on a qualitative plane. It matters not whether the number is 55 or 555, the real question is—even if the condemned men had shed blood, wouldn't it be better to avoid spilling more of it?

The history of abolition of the death penalty features Maximilien Robespierre as one of its stellar exhibits. The statement is attributed to him, "And what do they seek to show by the example? That one should not kill. And how do you teach that killing is wrong? By killing." Despite the label "the indestructible one," Robespierre was responsible for thousands of executions before being guillotined himself.

Would it not be better to renounce violence, including for even greater reason, legal violence? This is the agonistic question of Javier Arzuaga, dumbfounded by death.

This book does not deal with Che Guevara, except tangentially. Nor is it about the condemned men per se, even if it profiles several of them. Rather than addressing the lives of particular men, it regards human existence in general—as reflected in the life of each individual human being who wishes to be respected in his or her own right to exist. That is to say, we should resist death not only as a physical matter, but oppose it in a metaphysical fashion as well. This internal torment brought Javier Arzuaga to the brink of a nervous breakdown. As his father was dying, in May of 1959 he left La Habana and returned to the Basque Country. He was then reassigned as a Franciscan missionary in Peru, Ecuador, and Colombia.

Arzuaga's final posting was Puerto Rico. It was there that he left the priesthood and married. The couple lived together on the island for many years before moving, quite recently, to Atlanta, Georgia, to be near a son who was a nuclear engineer there.

*At Midnight* is a thorough self-analysis by its author. Javier Arzuaga's story parallels that of Miguel de Unamuno's character Manuel Bueno—a Catholic priest who doubted the existence of God, but who believed that religious faith was beneficial since it conferred the hope of salvation from the void that confronts us all. Javier, like the Unamuno's protagonist, lives the conflict between faith and reality that can only be described as agonistic. He invokes for the condemned men the resurrected Christ as proof of the immortality of the soul, in the attempt to achieve that men who are living as if they are about to die, die as if they are going to live forever. He admits at times that his own faith was shaky and his tenacity fruitless, yet he continued to believe that it was comforting for the condemned to believe in a future life in order to alleviate their immediate lot in this one. Javier is the doubting man of faith, who, paradoxically, cannot allow the intensity of his doubt to transcend that of his faith. It is the tragic sense of life of one who vacillates between faith and reason, reality and desire. This is the basis of Javier's actions and writings—the sense that gave meaning to his own personal odyssey.

This book was published in a first edition that displeased its author. Álvaro Vargas Llosa, and his political promoters in Miami, published it with the specific objective of discrediting Che Guevara. As part of that effort, they changed Arzuaga's title of the work (*A la media noche*, translated as *At Midnight*) to *Cuba 1959: La galera de muerte.*

Javier vacillated over the dissemination of his testimony, conscious that it could be easily manipulated in the international political climate of the day—dominated as it was by the law of the strongest (a nuclear arms race) and a planetary Cold War. At the same time, the memory of the executions at La Cabaña was as much a part of his being as was his spleen. Despite the fact that it awakened unpleasant old ghosts, he could not resist correcting and rewriting the text, at times making it more explicit and at others adding heart-breaking poems. Even with the changes, he had reservations about publishing his text, although he did want it to become available on the Internet. He did find it appealing to reissue this personally sincere and accurate new edition that was free of political manipulation. He did not live to see it in print.

The gunpowder bellowed,
the iron and stone howled
at midnight
in the moat of the laurels.
All the clocks suddenly stopped,
gently and in silence,
time itself prepared to stop.
One by one the stars went out,
the moon was engulfed by a black veil.
The sky opened up and space ceased to exist.
Neither right nor left,
neither up nor down,
neither inside nor outside.
Everything still, nothing moved,
the walls and the trees lost in the haze,
fear hovering like a cloud.
Ghosts filled La Cabaña.
We were a ballet of ghosts,
directed by Death.
From emptiness to emptiness,

silence to silence.
At midnight.

# 1

I am Javier Arzuaga Lasagabaster. The surnames say it all, but just in case anyone is in any doubt, I'll spell it out. I'm Basque on all four sides. I was brought into this world in Oñati, Gipuzkoa, exactly eighty-two years and fifty days ago. I am an ex-priest, I think I still belong to the Catholic Church, and I'm married to Stella Andino Padilla. We've raised three children: Xabi, Madalen, and Maite. Mother and children, all four of them, are Puerto Rican, and proud of it, they declare. I'm pleased they are. It's good to know and understand where we come from.

My parents were really "good people," great people. And I don't know whether I care if that had a lot or little to do with the fact that they were "children of their times." They were, above all else, firm Roman Apostolic Catholics and traditionalists (as opposed to liberals and/or republicans). "For God, for the Fatherland, and for the King." My father left us in time to miss seeing his children jump the fence and desert both fatherland and king. Not God, although maybe a little; but I'd say more than a little those who believe in and claim to represent God.

My parents fully obeyed the biblical instruction "be fruitful and multiply." They were poor, but what more can you give; he who said "multiply" can also multiply loaves of bread. They had eight children, although the last two girls died at an early age. However, I am sure my parents would not have complained if all six of their sons and daughters (four and two) had opted to remain celibate and wrap themselves in the habits of monks and nuns. A small contradiction that they would not, surely, have appreciated. (I have often said that my mother would have been a great, although short in stature, abbess of cloistered nuns). At home, we prayed more than in many convents. It's true, I know what I'm talking about. It was not a question of good or bad prayers, just that we prayed. And there was singing because my father was a musician, an organist and conductor of the parish choir and the municipal band. By age four, his six children played well the raised scale do-re-mi-fa-sol-la-ti-do and the lowered scale do-ti-la-sol-fa-mi-re-do. We also used to play, and played hooky from school on the odd afternoon even though I was an altar boy. We were never allowed to go near the movie theater, which I don't recall whether it was called Aloñamendi; no, not that, because the Pope used to say something along the lines of: "from movies to hell."

I was ten-years-old when I was sent to the Franciscan seminary in Arantzazu, which at that time we called Aránzazu. At the age of ten no child knows whether he has been called by God or not to the "religious life," I did not know whether I had any vocation or not. My parents certainly did for me, and in a big way. In my adolescence I felt, on more than one occasion, the desire to give up my studies and return home. I used to cry and bite my tongue, because how could I do that to my parents? Forget it, don't even think about it, get on with it. God will provide. Idiot, worse than an idiot! God didn't provide anything, no guidance or spiritual teacher that told me: "come on, this is not your vocation, go home." The vocation my parents felt for me never entered or dwelled in my heart. I hid it, I kept quiet, I did what I could. And the years went by. I should never have been ordained a priest. I should never have taken vows in the Franciscan order, they should never have sent me to the seminary at age ten. In August 1967 I preached my last mission, in Peru, specifically in Chaclacayo, near Lima, where the road leaves the coastal plain and begins to climb into the Andes. That afternoon, the archbishop cardinal of Lima had severely reprimanded me because he had received complaints along the lines of "look at what that priest says in his sermons." But he was not the inspiration behind my words that night. I still don't understand today, nor will I ever understand, why, on what basis, I said at the beginning of my intervention, from the pulpit and to a packed church—I remember it as if it were yesterday: "I am the cadaver of a child I killed—or they killed—when I was ten years old." Terrible, I don't understand. It is, was, just a sentence, a bad sentence. I'm no killer nor have I been killed. In 1959, in Cuba, I would not have spoken so crudely or brutally.

When the Latin grammar was placed in front of me and I began to memorize *musa*, *musae*, and *dominus*, *domini*, and the *ego sum*, *tu es*, I wasn't stupid, nor a genius; I simply realized I didn't like studying and that I was always going to be a bad student. A bad student, but a good reader whenever a short story, a poem, or a novel came my way. Five years of what was termed "humanities," then, aged fifteen, my novitiate, followed by three years of philosophy, and, to finish up, four of theology. Thirteen years in all. They were years of and following the Spanish Civil War and World War II. Very difficult years of hunger, of isolation, of false smiles, of emaciated dreams, of hidden, silent, and buried hatreds, of fears. Franco abhorred and persecuted all things Basque, the language, the practices and customs, because he identified them with separatism. Many of the Franciscans, for their part, did not used to hide their feelings as passionate enthusiasts of all things Basque—practices, customs, and the language. We kept out of politics. Yet books of many different stripes came our way, with no origin or destination, and were handed around under the table. We were allowed to speak about soccer, pelota, cycling, sports—substitutes for politics. We finished our degrees more or less trained in theology and completely uninformed when it came to politics and social questions. I had no idea why they were lumped together.

(A friend told me years later that he asked the person in charge of our spiritual training during those years we were studying theology why he mistreated me, why he didn't trust me at all, why he didn't show me the least bit of respect, and he replied that I wasn't devout, that I didn't take my spiritual formation seriously. Yeah! But why didn't he filter me out in time?)

When it came time to distribute us to our respective destinations, it was suggested that I go to Rome to study liturgy and Gregorian chant and similar musical things, even though they grated on my ears, and then return to Arantzazu, to direct the choir for life, yikes, no, no, impossible. Wasn't there anything else? If not that, then Cuba. Great, then Cuba it was. That was when I began to open my eyes. There were four of us, all four recently hatched, and, with the provincial father's knowledge and blessing, we were going to be put, without even a lousy *peseta* for anything unforeseen, into the hold of an old rundown ship that was ready to wave goodbye to the seas to be broken up for scrap. I went to ask him for a travel allowance for the four of us. The ticket was all-inclusive, he replied. Something had to be done, and I muttered into my holy habit. I found a way of making four thousand pesetas "fall"—stealing sounds so ugly, right—into my hands. That, in the end, didn't get us anything, and the provincial father fell out with me forever. My eyes were opened a little more when I believed myself to have been unfairly treated when denied just two days to be with my family before undertaking the journey—my companions had enjoyed seven—and I fled the monastery for a day, which could have cost me dearly. The trip continued to open my eyes. But in what Old Testament cave had we been living, my God! And just a few hours after setting foot in Havana they were opened up as wide as two moons on a translucent night when I was informed I was going to have to teach the *Ezpatadantza* (sword dance), a Basque folkloric dance, at the National Ballet School of Cuba, run by the Alonso family (Alicia and Alberto). Only I know how much I enjoyed myself in doing so (well, I guess that's not true, because I've just told you). And if anyone, while smirking, wants to think the worst, I would clarify that it was not there that I lost my innocence and my virginity.

My assigned destiny in Cuba was to play the organ in the Church of San Antonio on Fifth Avenue in Miramar, but someone else went there instead, so I had to fill the vacancy that had been left open in the Santiago de las Vegas seminary. The superior of the house was concerned about my dance classes and the atmosphere in the ballet school, so one day he asked me to take a stroll with him up and down the soccer field. He began to speak about saving my soul, which he saw to be under serious threat, and, well, he wanted to lend a hand. Of course, me fraternizing with guys and girls, and the latter so underdressed . . . he had to look out for me, shield me. He recommended that I be entrusted to Mother Sister Something, founder of some likewise unknown congregation, whose beatification process was moving ahead and required a miracle. He asked me to pray a novena to her and . . . yes, clearly, he was right, yes, yes, of course. Such nonsenses, and they call them spiritual direction.

A Latin and Spanish teacher; they could equally have assigned me to teach geography and history. Not the sciences. Not mathematics nor physics or chemistry. I wasn't made for the sciences, and gave up on them from day one. In reality I wasn't cut out for teaching either. I realized that in the first year: I would never be a good teacher, because I was undisciplined and impatient. But those four years in Santiago de las Vegas were not at all bad.

On the contrary. I gave my classes, I had time to read, and there was no shortage of books on quite a wide spectrum of topics and authors. The soccer balls were not made of rags and there was a big swimming pool filled with cool water. We ate very well. We lived on a ranch in the country. I took part now and again in the agricultural endeavors, like cutting through rock thirty feet deep until reaching an underground water source. In the third year I had to take part as an assistant in a missionary campaign in parishes close to the seminary, which led me to meet families who accepted me into their own lives. Two of those friendships, still so dear, continue half a century later. Out of these first missionary initiatives came my commitments to look after two Catholic Action groups.

Without even realizing it, my readings and contacts with normal people gradually taught me what my studies had not: about the world in which we live. Before it was a sinful world that had to be redeemed. Now I was learning to regard injustice and poverty as the most serious of sins. From our vantage point as men of the Church, sheltered from the world, we could not appreciate in their full reality and meaning the forces that clashed in a complex and confusing Field of Agramante: laws, socialism, rights, Moscow, Rome, Washington, dynamite, peace conferences . . . First they were just tickles, then scratches, and I ended up thinking more about social justice than "eternal truths."

It was very sketchy, still quite immature, a badly seasoned, half-cooked dish. But I liked it; I really got into it.

Before they assigned me to the parish of Casa Blanca, I had seen, like a bolt of lightning, the remnants of my vocation go up in flames. A phantasmagoric vision that came and went. The product of unresolved old doubts and the frenzy of the new moment. I closed my eyes again like an ostrich. Nor did I stop to consider if my first religious and theological doubts were endangering my faith. I considered them to be quite normal, I told myself that the abnormal thing would be to not ask myself any questions, not to doubt. I remembered something that I had read in some book or heard someone say. Namely, that the truth that comes out of doubt is that which is most firmly established. And my thoughts were similar when I felt something stirring in my emotional life. It had a name. Huh! I recalled Saint Anthony, Saint Francis of Assisi, other saints. If they were tempted, what was so strange about me being so as well?

"I don't consider myself prepared to assume responsibility for the parish, I have absolutely no experience at all," I replied to the provincial delegate when he summoned and informed me of his intention to transfer me to the San Francisco monastery in Old Havana in order to attend to the parish of Casa Blanca. I told him that because I thought it was right to do so, humbly and imbued with good will. He advised me not to worry, that it was a very small parish and I would figure it out in no time at all. There are things that are more important than size. And there are abilities and capacities that can't be improvised or that, if they are, are never quite right. I knew this and yet, under the auspices of misguided humility, I was happy they had considered me. Of course I felt able to do this and more. And one fine day in the month of October, exactly four years after setting foot on Cuban soil at Quay No. 1 in the Port of Havana, I was presented to the neighborhood directly opposite that port on the other side of the bay, to the Franciscans of the Good Counsel and to five people—like the five fingers on a hand—who were in effect the directing-hand of the parish of Casa Blanca.

I soon came to realize that my affinity with the faithful of Casa Blanca was limited and inadequate, and that there was little room for improvement with the majority of the population, the very poor. The people in Casa Blanca were simple, friendly, and kind, but reserved and not too disposed toward priests and churches. They were more on the impoverished and unschooled end of the social spectrum; not the well-educated middle-class. They were Catholic, profoundly Catholic, twice a year, the evening of Good Friday during the procession of the Crucifixion of Christ and his Mother of Sorrows, and on the evening of July 16, during the procession of Our Lady of Mount Carmel, their patron saint. With their Panama hats and cigarettes hanging from their mouths, neither of which they removed. I got used to not stopping to greet or speak to anyone on my way from the ferryboats to the church and from the church to the ferryboats. Nor did they do so to me. A "hello," "hello," on passing by one another was more than enough.

The regular churchgoers, those that went to Sunday Mass, parents with children at the parish school, were somewhat more outgoing, but not by much. Their faith was rudimentary, riddled with superstitions. Those who responded to invitations to form dedicated lay groups and enlisted in one of the branches of the Acción Católica Cubana (ACC, Cuban Catholic Action) showed reasonably good will in the long term more or less; I managed to interest them in forming groups and demonstrating their faith without any qualms—in energizing the parish community. It was much more difficult for me to stimulate any interest in reading a good book. There were barely half a dozen lay militants with whom I could maintain any kind of intelligent conversation. Only a handful of people enjoyed my friendship and trust; very few and always with a touch of jealousy. I was very careful not to show any favoritism toward any one in particular. For a while at least, because over time I preferred certain circles and that relationship grew and grew into something elevated to a higher level and degree than mere friendship. In three years I only set foot in three homes. Once, only once, I was called on to attend to a dying man. Nor was there any funeral parlor in Casa Blanca. Apparently they took people away when they got really sick, at death's door.

I never paid the proper attention to my responsibilities. I accepted tasks, conscious of the fact I could not attend to them adequately, such as at first being on the Diocesan Board of the JOC's (*Juventud Obrera Católica*, Young Catholic Workers) women's section, and, later, on the Diocesan Board of the JAC's (*Juventud Acción Católica*, Young Catholic Action) men's section. The multiplication of these new and more time-consuming commitments did not rid my mind or heart of the whirlwind that was forming at the top, in the middle, and a little further down in my person.

The basic problem was vocational. Day by day I was becoming more firm in my conviction that I had never had one; no calling for either the religious life or the priestly ministry. No, it wasn't a question of losing or abandoning it. Reviewing the past, analyzing it without any preconceptions or too zealously, all the signs along the way from start to finish underscored that it came from others, beginning with my parents, who experienced the vocation through me and inculcated in me the calling. And now there were only two options left for me. I could turn back the clock or invent a substitute vocation. That is, I could try to live as if I were a member of a religious order with its three vows; a priest tied to the altar, to the pulpit, and to the confessional. The former was impossible, because of my parents. Neither he nor she, could take the blow; abandoning my vocation would kill them. Also, how would it look to my superiors and colleagues; what would they think and say about me? A huge idiot and a coward. So, without telling anyone, without daring to discuss my failure with anyone and biting the bullet, I carried on.

There I was lacking the water to irrigate the plot of my faith and full of torrents of questions and doubts. During my third year in Casa Blanca, my faith was a flag that began to come apart at the seams; it was in tatters. The Church as an institution—its origins, its history, the cumulative and corrupt power in the Vatican, the hierarchy, its lifestyles so at odds with the Gospel . . . with every passing day I believed in it less. There was no denying, on the other hand, the distinguished group of saints and the marvelous examples of the devotion of priests, as well as bishops, members of religious orders, and laypersons to the noblest causes of loving one's neighbor, and the contributions to civilization, to culture, and to the arts that have germinated within the Church. I had more questions and doubts about doctrines on grace and sin and sacraments. I abhorred, for example, sitting in the confessional and dispensing absolution: the "I absolve you." And don't even mention the beliefs we had been taught regarding hell, heaven, purgatory, and limbo. I did not refute anything, but the doubts grew and became more of a challenge within me. Theology, dogmas, had been invented by theologians in their workshops, I told myself, marvelous craftsmanship of thought and explanation, but inventions. God and Jesus of Nazareth and Saint Mary were still untouchables for me, at least for the moment. They remained the fundamental, the nucleus, the most important, the essential.

My feelings were also in crisis. Inevitably, it had to happen. They don't exist apart; they are a part of the whole and the whole was in crisis. I fell in love with a woman and convinced myself that women and men are complimentary; that they need one another. Whirlpools and eddies and riptides. We suffered together while letting our riverbed run dry. But later new rains and new waters came to flow and to sing therein.

I was the parish priest of Casa Blanca for three years. For the first two of those, Batista was in power while Fidel and his people were in the Sierra Maestra. The whole of Cuba lived on edge, as people say, during those two years. In Casa Blanca there was a very particular heartbeat, due to the influence that the La Cabaña military encampment exercised over the local population. There were a lot of military or police families, some retired, but many others on active duty. That forced me to speak and act with caution—and not a little annoyance. I had to respect the opinions of everyone. And for that reason I had to keep quiet, keep my own ideas and political preferences to myself. It was difficult for me because in other contexts I could speak out and express myself openly, without holding back. These were the other scenarios in which I operated, especially the diocesan boards regarding Catholic Action on which I was a counsellor. Moreover, in the community to which I belonged, there was much talk about news that originated from one source or another. Sympathy mostly inclined toward the rebels, due in the main to the fact that we Basques —almost all the Franciscans in Cuba were of Basque origin—had the thorn of the Franco dictatorship in our side and, given their similarities, detested all dictatorships. In the San Francisco monastery and other Franciscan centers in Havana it was not uncommon to hide people on the run because of their ideas or their antigovernment activities—those who ran the risk of being arrested, jailed, tortured, and eliminated. José Antonio Echeverría and Juan Pedro Carbó Serviá, leaders of the student movement and of the civil resistance, both anti-Batista revolutionary movements, hatched a plan to storm the Royal Palace while in hiding in the San Francisco monastery. They left there to take part in the bloody battle in which Echeverría perished and Serviá escaped with his life, only to die soon afterward in an ambush.

The police knew about the situation of the monastery because it was long-standing and serviced equally those of one political leaning as those of its opponents, united as they were in their repressed political status and therefore in opposition to the regime. It was a kind of political asylum. There is no way that the authorities had or could have had information in each particular case. On one occasion, shortly before the dictator fled, one of the heads of Catholic Action approached me to say that a police official, a friend of the family, had spoken in his home about the possibility of a search of the San Francisco monastery being carried out by the authorities because they suspected that several revolutionaries were hiding out there. He trusted the guy and assured me that he was not leading us into a trap. That night, when I got home, I brought my superior up to speed on what I had been told. He met with Echeverría and Servía and they decided to leave the monastery immediately. My superior asked me if I would be willing to take them to Santiago de las Vegas—not to the seminary, but to the retreat house. I occasionally let myself be carried away by a spirit of adventure and that night was one of those occasions. We left at ten at night, conscious of the fact that we could arrive safely or fall along the way. We made it. Later it turned out that there was no search of the monastery.

I believed in Fidel Castro and his people with an unshakeable faith. I believed that his revolutionary ideas and projects were clean; that, in effect, Cuba would awaken to a better life when the mountains descended to the lowlands and his ideas elevated cities and towns. I thought the mountain guerrillas would embrace those in the civilian resistance and together they would form one common front, and that days of justice and peace were approaching. I did not see the official Church as particularly mixed up or involved in the task, although I did when it came to lay Catholics. I knew that among their ranks there were well-trained leaders seeking to contribute ideas and unconditional enthusiasm. I was anxious for their day to arrive.

You are all rock
Castillo de San Carlos de La Cabaña.
Rock on the outside and rock on the inside,
rock on the tortured earth,
rock under the deep dark sky.
Rock is your root,
rock your blood and your time,
rock your space,
rock your vigil and your slumber.
Rock the water of your rain,
rock your light and your wind.
Rock your voices,
rock your feelings.
Rock the air that flows into your walls
I breathe and I smell.
Rock the shout that I hear,
rock your knives and the pain I feel.
Rock our bitter weeping,
rock our silence.
Stand up this morning,

catacomb of my rocky memories,
stand up, rock of La Cabaña,
to observe your dead pass by.

# 2

January 1, 1959 came and triggered the big party. Cuba had just been born for the third time. Serve the champagne, waiter, we're going to celebrate. Bottles of sparkling wine were opened and fizzed in abundance. But the biggest revelation and most intoxicating effervescence was that of the soul of the Cuban people. Some because they had fought for freedom and they saw that the day had come on which they could celebrate, others because the joy and enthusiasm were contagious and spread like wildfire, everyone taking to the streets and shouting and singing and dancing in an indescribable revolutionary fever. They were praising Fidel Castro, July 26, the rebel army, the "bearded ones" and their weapons in their hands and their rosaries around their necks. It all lasted days and weeks and months until, worn out, the soul of the Cuban people calmed down and swore loyalty to the new order: the Revolution. The odyssey of the struggle for power had come to an end. With the hated, bastard, sergeant dictator having fled, his army defeated on land, at sea, and in the air, Fidel Castro became the new sole owner of Cuba.

Cuba was born for the third time. Five hundred years previously, a little less, it doesn't matter, it was begotten as a colony of Spain. It occupied a privileged geographical position on which a people gradually developed and created its own culture, its economy, its dreams of being free of any overlords. In 1898, and again in 1902, a partial independence was born through emancipation first from Spain and then from the United States, which wanted Cuba as a colony, in like manner as Puerto Rico and the Philippines. Partial because it fell into the grip of political interests that battered it badly for almost sixty years. Free elections and democratic governments that were interrupted by three military coups, with their usual periods of dictatorships, in a little more than half a century didn't make for a very appealing independence. Now the sun of justice was truly rising, poverty and ignorance would be eradicated, peace was appearing for the first time, and Cuba was being born definitively into a decent independent life.

It was reasonable to celebrate it. I joined in the general jubilation without anyone forcing me to do so. I shouted and sang until my voice went and I carried on jumping up and down and expressing my enthusiasm and mixing with the people in the streets and squares until I collapsed exhausted. That was a Thursday. When the first bearded guys from Escambray showed up on Friday and Saturday in military jeeps and trucks requisitioned from the Santa Clara and Matanzas barracks, accompanying Camilo Cienfuegos and Che Guevara, Havana welcomed them like superheroes, like mythological cyclopes that had rescued Cuba from the depths of the ocean. There were no military parades. There were no speeches. The speechmaker was Fidel, and he had already embarked, in Santiago de Cuba, on the biggest and noisiest triumphal march in history—greater than that of Julius Caesar on his return to Rome from the Gallic Wars, ten days in suspense, without any rest, until the military encampment in Columbia was taken. And the celebration continued in Havana without any interruption or waning until the supreme invincible leader arrived.

On Sunday, the 4th, I found myself in Casa Blanca faced with a different reality. I was expecting it; it had to be that way. I saw some faces full of joy and weariness, and others worried and fearful, and I made note of those I didn't see or would ever see again. Casa Blanca had always been influenced by nearby La Cabaña, the military base that seemed to ride piggy- back upon it. A weight that used to crush it. There were few regular churchgoing families that didn't include active or retired military personnel or police officers. I wouldn't have expected them to be too happy about seeing their parish priest identified with a revolution that was defining itself in radical antimilitarist terms, and that was announcing judicial measures against those that, in one form or another, had defended the dictatorship and, by virtue of that defense, had participated in blood crimes that had, to be sure, been quite frequent and cruel in recent years. I was conscious of that and I was worried. As parish priest, I had a duty to everyone equally, without any distinctions or preferences or rejections of any kind. It was expected of priests to not be members of any political party or movement, but in reality it was hardly natural to expect us not to have any political thoughts or preferences. It was a dilemma. I said to myself in all seriousness: "Javier, keep your mind alert, your mouth shut, and be careful."

La Cabaña presented an additional problem that, whether I liked it or not, I would have to confront. The fortress of San Carlos in La Cabaña was within the parish limits of Casa Blanca. I didn't expect the new owners of the military base to call on my services more than had the previous ones. Already that first Sunday they didn't send the jeep that used to collect me at 10:00 a.m. and take me up to the chapel of Santa Bárbara. Someday I'd have to go up there and greet the new man in charge who, it was rumored, could be—if he wasn't already—the Argentinian doctor Ernesto Che Guevara. I'd explain to him the custom of holding

Mass and he'd attend to me with whatever was at his disposal. But there was another matter, that of the prison, the resounding prison of La Cabaña. The prisoners were also my parishioners. As far as I knew, no one representing the parish of Casa Blanca had ever visited the prison or offered their services to its inmates. I had asked for authorization or a visitor's pass in my position as parish priest and chaplain when the governor of the fort was Fulgencio Batista's brother-in-law, and my request had been denied. I would have to ask once again. Possibly, I told myself, permission would be denied again. Should the answer be yes, well, it was better not to think about that until whatever call that had to be made was made. The alarm bells were already going off. I'd just have to see.

For the moment, I'd keep my feet on the ground, I wouldn't go with either side, neither the winners nor the losers. I would be prudent, more prudent than I had been during those first three days of the triumph of the revolution. That night or the next day or the one after that, at a moment now lost to me in the mist of time, an idea entered my mind, penetrated it, took hold of it. It forced me to consider very real the notion that the Gospel prohibited me from being neutral, which obliged me to prefer the neediest, the sick, the persecuted, the imprisoned, and to reserve for that purpose the best part of me, my best dedication, my best service. I tried to set aside that budding authenticity and generosity. When had I ever caught sight within me before any similar type of obedience to the Gospel within me? It was ridiculous. One thing was fulfilling my duty and another was overstepping the mark in the role of a cheap fraud—a clown.

A swarm of rumors was spreading through the streets. The television stations stopped being governed by schedules and preexisting shows, they were a real hubbub of improvisations in the studios and in the streets. It was the same with the radio. The newspapers appeared like volcanoes of news without any control, burning lava. They all wanted to be the first to transmit Fidel's march and his speeches. The caravan proceeded slowly, stopping in every town, at every crossroads, where people from the interior were waiting to acclaim the leader and Fidel talked and talked and talked, but that was it, this guy had ever taut bowstrings, he was a miracle of stamina. He didn't fulfill that role of the smart guy for whom few words are enough. Both good and bad smart guys became equally drenched under the waterfall of his endless verbosity. Fidel never paused in order to think. His was a torrential rain. You sink or swim.

Certain key points of understanding could, however, be discerned clearly. Greater insistence on certain points became flags behind which to rally, announcements of what was to be expected. There were three bundles or rolls of ideas that would soon come to be the key foci of action or starting points. I'm speaking for myself, what I appeared to see, what stood out for me. First: promises and hopes. The revolution was for the historically disinherited, the poor. They could be assured that their thirst would be quenched, their wishes fulfilled, the land would be theirs, from being the forgotten they would become the privileged. It almost sounded like evangelical bliss. And how big would that "almost" be? Second: friends and enemies. The revolution was passion, love, dedication. It didn't want lukewarm indifferent people, those that moved between two sides, like me for instance. You were either with it or against it. Now, the enemy could be sure that they would be persecuted and exterminated. The great enemy began to take shape on the horizon, the one who would soon take the stage or be placed on it; the tormentor to the north, the source of all evil, the United States. Third: justice. The revolution was justice. As punishment or prize. According to on whom it fell or for what purpose it served, justice would be the sword that the revolution held in its right hand. In conceiving its new laws of agrarian reform or education, and the revolutionary courts and their procedings, justice would become the source of inspiration.

There was more than enough means for the worried to express their concerns. Free cans of black paint were provided to anyone who chose to see everything in dark terms. There was more than enough meat for the talents of anyone seeking to insert into the events the scalpel of analysis and correction. Castro gave enough scope for anything. Initially, I trusted and hoped that the Revolution would take the right direction and not abuse the absolute power that had fallen into its hands.

Where I wait for the ferry,
leaning on a wall,
I observe the bank,
where Casa Blanca lives and sleeps.
There to the left,
on the ocean waves that break on the rocks,
the castle of the Reyes del Morro
and the lighthouse,
facing the ocean.
Opposite,
the fortress of San Carlos de La Cabaña
and the monument of Cristo de La Habana,
looking at us, at the city.
Symbol and synopsis
of Cuban history.
How completely shitty.
A history of conquests,
of blood and death,
of ambitions, hatreds, and injustices,
and a cement Christ

that blesses it and makes it Christian.
And the good things,
truth, justice, love,
which Christ in the flesh
taught us?
Thus, five hundred years ago.
Thus, one hundred years ago.
Thus, fifty years ago . . .
Thus, yesterday and thus, today.
It's sickening.
Until when, Lord?

# 3

January sixth, the Epiphany, the three holy wise men. They came from the east bearing gifts. Their names were Melchior, Caspar, and Balthazar. Or Che, Camilo, and Fidel? Who doesn't think that there were many, even countless, people in Cuba that thought this was all full of allegory, that all six were following the same star, and announcing salvation. And that they were giving gifts to those that had brought the Cuban people the revolution. We continued to celebrate endlessly. "Las campanas de Belén" (The bells of Bethlehem) and similar carols blended with other hymns and salutations. It would be different a year later when, unmasked and free of slogans, they said the three wise men were too many, and that one Fidel was sufficient. But that January sixth all this was still distant, part of the shadowy future. It wouldn't surprise me at all if, by some form of magic, the sorcerer pulled out of his sleeve a recording of something I said in my sermon that day to the effect that the revolution was the best Epiphany gift that God could have bestowed, and indeed did bestow, on us.

The day dawned and I made my way, like every day, to the ferries. La Cabaña opposite, surly as ever; would they come for me today to go and say Mass? What about Caridad and her family, would they still be living there? What would La Cabaña be like? I had never been inside the walled enclosure. It clearly had to smell of old stones soaked by rainwater and cured by the sun, indifferent to whoever was the owner today but gone tomorrow, loyal only to themselves and that rock on which they sat. What a lesson, ladies and gentlemen, what a lesson! The water was calm, it greeted, caressed, and the fingers of the breeze were soft, cool. It was going to be a beautiful Epiphany. The gift had already been given.

When I descended from the pulpit I hadn't decided yet what I was going to do that day— a stroll, a visit, the tranquility of home, a book, a movie perhaps in the evening? And suddenly, it didn't matter since, whether before or after the sermon, it came to me as if one of Melchior's pages was suggesting the idea: if the people in La Cabaña were not coming down for me, why don't I go up there to see what's going on? Or, what's more, maybe I should go along to the commanding officer's residence and ask to see Che Guevara? Would he welcome me? It became more difficult to concentrate. How would the commandant be in person? Would he let me look him in the eye? What kind of Marxist was he? Would we talk or would we argue?

I waited longer than usual. The military jeep didn't come to pick me up. Well, there would be no Mass for them today either. I left around mid-day, but, instead of going down to the ferryboats, I ascended the road carved out of the rock toward the gate of the fort. It was nice tropical winter weather, sunshine and an sea breeze. I was without any greeting card or prepared speech in order to introduce myself to the militiamen of the rebel army, to the official in charge. "Good day," I'd tell them when they'd order me to "halt." "I've come to say hello to Commander Guevara, may I?" In all likelihood they'd ask me, "And who are you?" "About what and why do you want to speak to the Commander?" "Well," I made a mental note, "my name is so and so and I'm the parish priest here, of Casa Blanca, and I'd like to see Che in person and shake his hand and thank him, if I may," I said to myself.

Not at all. From what I could see, the protocol that day was to let in whoever showed up, without asking for any names, without asking whether they were carrying any sharp weapons or firearms, without prying into the color of their eyes or the space below the drape of their eyebrows. "Do you know where you're going?" "To his residence." "But do you know where it is?" "Yes, turn left once you get to the top." "Well, have a good day." "Thank you." I walked past the feet of the Cristo de La Habana, the monument that you could see clearly from far away. Up close you had to really stretch your neck upward to catch a glimpse of the face, which can't have been too pleasant for the Argentinian, to have Him so nearby and personal. Militiamen passed me by, arms tucked under their rifle belts, displaying rosaries and medals, shouting and gesticulating. To the ferryboats, to Havana, to drink, to cut loose, to celebrate the triumph. "Won't you give me a rosary, eh, priest?" "Don't you have enough?" "But I don't have one of yours" "Another day."

In the past I once went to the residence of the commanding officer, Batista's brother-in-law, on the occasion of a baptism, and I chatted with him for a few minutes. On account of the baptism he gave me a small envelope with three hundred pesos inside. Well, very generous, ill-gotten gains, I thought. I'm going to spend this before I get my fingers burned and hand it over to the Poor Claire Sisters in the Lawton neighborhood in exchange for a lovely harmonium for the parish. When I asked him for another generous gesture, his authorization to attend to the prisoners in the prison within the walls of La Cabaña, he replied: "What? Prisoners you say? No, I'm afraid you're mistaken. There are only soldiers here." "Well some of those soldiers have told me there are also prisoners and occasionally the odd prisoner has made it known to me, via those same soldiers, his wish for me to visit him, him and all of them." "No way, you didn't understand." I was never able, in fact, to enter the famous centuries-old dungeons, dating from the time of the conquistadors who came from afar, witnesses to many atrocities and many deaths during the secessionist wars and later the time of Machado, Batista's first revolt, and over the last few years of his dictatorship. Goodness, if only the walls of La Cabaña could tell everything they had seen and heard, everything they knew . . .

I don't think that, within the entire perimeters of La Cabaña and El Morro, there are even a dozen trees sufficiently big enough to make some shade. Half of them surrounded the commanding officer's home, sheltering it from the sun, and from the curiosity of any neighbors or strangers. It was a haven of peace within the cacophony of the military base, even the din coming from nearby seemed far away. On one side or the other, amid the flowerbeds, a hammock should have been strung up to welcome home the warrior, a place where he could lie down and relax. I went up to the front door. "Well, the commanding officer is busy at the moment, you'll have to wait, I don't think he'll be long, come in and sit down." As friendly as that, natural and good-natured, but without letting go of his gun, his right hand on the weapon at all times. It must have been a habit, they must have gone to bed like that, as if the guns were their loved ones, their wives. I wouldn't have liked to live like that. I saw he was tired. "Yes, I have a vague idea of what a bed is, I've been sleeping for days curled up in a corner or seated and sometimes standing up." Propped up by his gun? That would have been it. A guy whose skin was weather-beaten by the sun and wind. I looked him over and he seemed to have been shaped by teachers and books and notebooks.

The door soon opened and out came a ruddy-faced, chubby little guy, somewhat uncertain in his stride, and with unfocussed eyes; he crossed the room and disappeared from view in the mid-day sun. The still open door funneled someone's angry snarls from within. "Go ahead, Father, you can go in, it's the commanding officer, he won't do anything to you," the soldier reassured me on seeing my little startle and hesitation. I got up and walked over; "can I come in?"

"The next time you suggest any business like today's I'll throw you in prison, you good-for-nothing profiteer." The Argentinian kept shouting: "a lazy good-for-nothing." He was standing up, leaning against the desk, both hands resting on it. His neck seemed like it was made up of stretched pieces of string, as if it were trying to break free from his shoulder blades. His lower jaw was frozen in defiance and covered with a coarse and patchy beard. Lips tensed, teeth visible, eyes bulging, unkempt black hair, face infuriated, he proclaimed: "Jerks, they'll be thinking nothing has changed around here, that they can play around with the revolution, they're going to be playing in hell instead, that's where they're going. Oh, but Father, what are you doing at the door? Excuse me, I didn't see you, come in, take a seat." I had almost turned into a pillar of salt. How can someone change from such ferocity to being so cheerful so quickly, from the tone of a knife-wielding murderer to that of a smooth charmer, from a hyena ready to slit a meek lamb's throat into the picture of kindness? Wow! The surprises Che had up his sleeve, truly what I least expected. I walked three steps over to the desk and held out my hand, we shook and smiled at each other. I sat down.

It was up to me to start the conversation; after all, I requested the meeting, although he had already spoken when he invited me to sit down. And it was he who began the informal exchange about who I was and what brought me to his office. A sounding-out conversation between two strangers, aided, however, by the tone of two old friends who meet up again after many years. "I assume you haven't come here to give me an Epiphany gift nor to place yourself at my disposal." He beamed, almost sardonically, sitting there in his executive chair, playing with the pencil in his hands. "Or just to see my face, to check out whether I'm as fierce as they say here and there?"

To meet him, to greet him, to ask a favor of him. He asked me about the origins of my last name, Arzuaga. "It's Spanish, clearly, but from which region?" "It's a Basque last name. I imagine Guevara is also Basque, right?" "Basque, yes sir, and centuries old and noble. And full of the misdeeds of feudal lords no doubt." He was not unaware of the topic. That of lords and their droit de seigneur. Nor of the Basques at that time and their dispute with Franco. I spoke to him about the Ladrón de Guevaras who subjugated my town, Oñati, for centuries, and recounted the odd anecdote. "You're not hoping I make up for the cruelties committed by my ancestors, if indeed they were so, right?" From one surprise to another, because I would never have imagined such a relaxed and insignificant conversation with Commander Guevara at a time when the revolution undoubtedly called for his complete dedication and he was working flat out on a thousand extremely urgent matters. A rest along the way, a parenthesis in order to catch his breath? Or something else?

"Well, I'm here, Commander, to see if you'll allow me to keep on coming to La Cabaña every Sunday morning to say Mass in the chapel of Santa Bárbara, and if you'll allow me to visit the prisoners. I understand that the prison was emptied on New Year's Day, but it's filling up again with new prisoners." To the first question, he gave an unequivocal "no," and, to the second, an equally categorical "yes," without any glimmer of doubt or the placing of any conditions. He asked me if during the dictatorship many soldiers attended Mass? "You know very well, Commander, that nowadays only soldiers in the Spain of National Catholicism go to Mass and take communion; here, there were something like a dozen or so women, some of their children, and the person in charge of the chapel, at the door, with his back turned to the pulpit and smoking—but soldiers? Not even by accident." "Well, as they're not going to come now either, and without the need on my prohibiting it, for the record, you can save some time by not having to come on Sundays to say Mass." He became quiet for a few seconds. Then, in a raised voice, almost shouting, he said: "We're going to do one thing—guard, come here." The rebel soldier and his rifle entered. "Yes, Commander." "Find out who was in charge of the chapel, of Santa Bárbara did you say? And its key, ask for it, and bring it to me today, without fail, I say. I'll personally throw it into the ocean."

He then went on to say solemnly, still smiling but at the same time firmly, slowly and resolutely pronouncing each word, as in a proclamation of principles and orders: "Here in La Cabaña, from now on, all Masses, catechisms, rosaries, anything smelling of religion, Christian, Muslim, or

Buddhist, among the corps of my soldiers, both in politics as well as in philosophy and religion, are abolished, strictly forbidden. Only I and those I appoint are in charge, only I will give the orders, is that clear?" "Clear, crystal clear." "And are you surprised, Father?" "Well, you know what? Surprised, not surprised exactly, no, but I would like to know why in the Sierra Maestra mountains you had a chaplain, Father Sardiñas, and in the last few months other chaplains in other mountain ranges?" "When we had them it was because we needed them, now we don't need them, so they're of no value, we're on the same page, right?" "Absolutely."

As regards the prison, after responding to his curiosity about what the previous owners of La Cabaña thought and how they acted—"Cruel, right?" he added mockingly, "to allow some poor defenseless prisoners to suffer in solitude without the assistance of a priest and to die without his solace or blessings, but the revolution is different"—he accepted the fact that the prison was filling up, that new occupants were showing up every day, that there was not going to be enough space given that there were many police officers and soldiers who had behaved badly and had to face trials. "You can visit them as much as you want, whenever you want, and for as long as you want." "Would you mind giving me written permission, something that would serve as a letter of safe-conduct? I don't want there to be . . ." "No, I can assure you it won't be necessary, you'll be able to come and go and move around inside as you please, and if anyone bothers you just let me know and we'll sort it out. I hope you don't do anything that would bar you from entering." Without me asking him for any further explanation, he offered it freely. He mentioned that soon the revolutionary justice trials would take place in La Cabaña. "Trials? Did you say *trials*?" "Yes, the revolutionary *trials*, because there is much to judge and a lot to be paid for." There would be executions, and for that reason an execution wall. He told me there would be a lot, an awful lot, of work to do; he advised me to get my vestments ready. "You're going to be needed, Father."

I thought that, having arrived at that point, the visit had ended and I could get up and say my goodbyes. "But, are you in a hurry? Why don't we carry on chatting a while?" He would be happy to exchange opinions on justice in the pages of the Gospel and in those of the two-thousand-year history of the Church that had dictated what was good and what was bad and had inspired more than anyone the doctrine and the guidelines that had dominated the social life we term civilized, western, Christian. Che was far from ignorant in the question of religion, and specifically the Christian variety. I did not ask him whether he studied religion to follow or to persecute it. According to him, the Gospel was a pure utopia, the Beatitudes a beautiful garden in the antipodes of reality, its promises words cast into the wind because they are based on something as ephemeral as the love of one's neighbor and because the selfish and the ambitious who abuse everyone else and accumulate all the wealth are not only not punished at that time, but end up becoming the owners of their fellow men and of the world.

His opinion of the Church was stronger still. It was a lie that it lived according to the Gospel that it preached; not even capable of putting into practice its own social doctrines. "No, Commander, you're wrong; there are many men and women in the Church who forget about themselves and join their fellow men in poverty and in any difficult period of pain." "Don't trick me, you know which church I'm talking about." It was at that point that I heard him refer for the first time to the "new man" that was going to emerge out of the revolution, the nameless revolution. I asked him, innocently, if he wasn't also inventing a new utopia. "Not even so new, because all that about the 'new man' is an old dream and you know it, Commander." Che was not interested in theories. The message he transmitted to me, put in the words of a bridge to reality, was diaphanous. The Church should be honest with itself and before society. It should acknowledge its failure. The world was still a mess. The Church should withdraw and leave some space for others to apply their principles and methods. If he, Che, didn't solve the problems, well, he'd withdraw and let someone else try, until someone got it right. Of course I don't remember the exact words he used, although I do recall quite clearly his ideas. "What a great thing, Commander! Neither you Marxists trust us Christians nor do we trust you. But I'm not sure. Perhaps the problem doesn't stem from just a lack of mutual trust and is rooted in something deeper, don't you think?" He wanted to tell me that he was not a Communist, that I could look in the party archives and in those of each of its cells and I would not find his name anywhere. I replied: "It's possible, and so what? You and I both know that we are what is in our mind and heart, not in some name on a list."

We said goodbye with a warm handshake and a "see you soon," both of us convinced we would continue to do so. On my walk back to La Cabaña and Havana I told myself that I would have to pick apart our conversation in detail to figure out Che's hidden intentions, because the commander was not being dishonest. But it did seem pretty clear that he was holding back on a lot of things. He had surprised me and I was flattered by his attention. I had more questions on descending than when I had gone up to see the commander.

A robot
neither loves nor hates, neither thinks nor
feels.
A robot obeys.
Go over there . . . and it goes, come here . . .
and it comes,
laugh . . . and it laughs, shut up . . . and it shuts
up,
kill . . . and it kills.
Will Marcial be turning out to be
a good robot for them?
He never asks "why?"
He simply obeys.
His face does not express
whether he thinks this is good, if he is happy,
whether he thinks that is bad, if he is upset.
Marcial shines, however, made from
good stock:
he has noble feelings,
upright criteria,

friendly, obliging, honest.
Is it that he's in the process
of becoming a robot?
Will Marcial be one of the "new men"
of whom Che dreamed about?

# 4

The doors were open. I could come and go freely, anytime I wanted and by whichever door I preferred, by the front entry coming up from Casa Blanca or by the back next to the mouth of the tunnel. I could come with a purpose or just to stroll through the open spaces, or walk along the walls and contemplate Havana from there or go visit the fortress El Morro. I could come on foot or by car. And nobody would bother me, that's what the boss, Che, had said. But right now, at the very moment that I was empowered, I began to feel—what inside? Unease, fear, repugnance? Inside. And on the 7th, a Wednesday, I told myself that the prison would still not be organized and so I didn't go, and on Thursday I gave myself some other excuse and didn't go either. And I called myself a coward. When I went to catch the ferry on Friday, I saw that La Cabaña and its rocks were laughing at me, and I felt worse.

It was part of my obligations, as parish priest of Casa Blanca, to offer my services to the parishioners that asked for them, as well as to anyone who might be in need of them. All the inhabitants of La Cabaña, including its commanding officer, were also my parishioners, whether they liked it or not. But was it my pastoral zeal or some other hidden interest camouflaged within him that led me to the residence of Commander Guevara? Did I really want to transmit solace and encouragement to the prisoners, or was I instead just seeking to be there and to be an eyewitness, to stimulate my glands and my neurons, eavesdropping on the fire and the abyss of the events that were being announced, of which Che himself had told me in advance? I knew myself, I knew that my intentions, wishes, and eagerness were like a multi-colored rainbow, that not everything was so pure, that my curiosity was as real as my apostolic zeal, although not so much. I had the feeling that matters would become tense, that I could come up against the unexpected. I could be taking something on that I wasn't strong enough to deal with. I didn't, of course, have the necessary imagination to see everything that was about to take place just round the corner, nor the heavy seas and turmoil into which I would find myself plunged. "Should I ask my superior to look for my replacement? No, maybe later."

Friday, January 9. It's now or never. After Mass and breakfast, I set out (finally!) on my way. The road snakes up from Casa Blanca in the form of a Z, one hundred meters, little more, in each straight section, at the starting point in the small town square. At the first bend, turning to the right, there is the access control point, at the second bend, turning to the left, the Christ of Havana, and at the place of arrival, on the very summit, the entrance to the camp. If you had to visualize its perimeters with your eyes closed, all you'd have to do is imagine the open palm of your left hand. The camp itself would extend to the point where the fingers begin, within in what was known as "Mount Venus," with residential buildings, a theater, warehouses, workshops, and the chapel, and, at the finger tips, El Morro. To the right of the palm, as far as the eye could see, was the Atlantic, and, to the left, the natural channel flowing out into the bay and the port of Havana. In the space occupied by the thumb was the castle of San Carlos de La Cabaña, the walled enclosure. The camp must have occupied in all a square kilometer, more or less.

I approached the bridge over the moat, the inner wall and the arched gateway. It looked like a medieval castle, although the fort was built much later, at the beginning of 1700. The moat ran from north to south, beginning at the foot of the prison and running toward a small square known as the "moat of the laurels" in which there was the execution wall that could be accessed by an entrance checkpoint on the first bend in the Z. Upon entering through the gateway one felt immediately both out of time and out of place, like an island but in reverse, a drop of water surrounded by rock on all sides except for the ceiling of the sky. I said to myself: "This is small, it's impossible to get lost here. If I go left, the street keeps on doubling back until it meets the other street parallel to it where the command headquarters is located, and beyond that is the wall. Here to the right and then at the rear, is the prison. You can see it from here. All the gateways face different offices or outbuildings."

"Where am I heading? I'm here to visit the prison, ok, but it's early, I'm not in a hurry. The prison was still an itch, but I resisted scratching it. Let's see what I come across in command HQ; not the new commanding officer, I'll bet." A small reception area was walled in dark wood, encircled by a bench, a wine-colored tile floor, a vaulted ceiling, just one window, two or three pictures on the walls, and the door to the commanding officer's office. The Cuban coat of arms hung on the front wall, and there was a big, long, shiny uncluttered desk made out of fine wood, with comfortable chairs on both sides—for the staff no doubt. It was occupied at that moment by two officials, strange specimens in the uniform of the defeated army, quite dapper and all the more strange for that, like fish out of water. "We're in a transition, and, of course, it will be like this for a few days, the new commanding officer came once, we don't know if he'll be in charge here, what are we to do? Stay, wait, nothing." They didn't want to speak, good idea, loose lips sink ships. There are silences and attitudes that scream out disillusionment and helplessness. "We never get to leave here, except for the break," they smiled sadly, "we lean out from over there on the balcony of the wall to look at the breakwater and the ocean."

I went out there as well. The view was truly spectacular. In the prison they didn't know I was coming, they were not expecting me, I'd go there soon. The officials were right. It must have been really beautiful at night. The mouth of the port was at your feet, the port to the left, straight ahead the city, the archbishop's residence, the cathedral, the old San Francisco monastery next to Quay No. 1, Old Havana, up above the Capitol, the Galician Center. Descending by way of the Paseo del Prado you reached the breakwater, the white foam of breaking waves all along it, the Vedado neighborhood there in the distance, the blue, blue, blue of the ocean with a brushstroke of silver, the sun's reflections, in which your eyes got lost. I would return to this spot many times after coming out of the prison or back from the courts or the execution wall.

Slowly, I approached the prison, the big steel doors painted a garish green, somewhat flamboyant. A buzzing noise resembling that of a beehive increased the closer I got; it was coming from the courtyard and it made itself heard above the walls and outside the bars. A group of women were punching with their fists the steel plates, in vain, shouting, in vain, crying, in vain, no one attending to them, no one paying them any attention. It was a depressing scene to me: the huge ugly main door, the women shouting, the indifference of the militiamen coming and going. I went up to the first one who was walking toward the door. "Hey there, tell the official in charge that the priest of Casa Blanca wants to come in, that I have authorization from Commander Guevara."

"Father, Father. Are you going to see the prisoners?" One of the ladies came up to me. "Do me a favor, ask about my husband, Captain XX, tell him that . . " Without realizing it, the women had crowded around me. "Mine is called XX, I need him to tell me where he left the papers about . . " "Lieutenant XX, Father, Lieutenant XX, his mother's about to die . . " All of them at the same time, all in a rush, without any kind of references, descriptions, or ways of telling who their husbands, brothers, sons, boyfriends were. "It's not going to be possible like this, put it to me in writing." When the guards opened the door and invited me in, a few seconds later, I understood my new function as mailman or errand boy, which would come to the fore in the days ahead. I didn't like it one bit, just thinking about it was worrying enough.

Now I was in the prison of La Cabaña. What I saw, however, at first glance, was a huge iron-barred cage, including iron bars on top, a security space between the street and the courtyard. It was where all the hopes of anyone entering handcuffed died and in which those of anyone leaving a free man were reborn. On the other side of the railings, in the courtyard, was a swarm of men wearing blue jeans, a large P on the backs of their prison jackets, some strolling around, others still, in groups; the buzzing of the beehive. At the edges of the courtyard were the black caves, with the galleries, also enclosed in iron bars, ten for bedrooms, three for a storeroom, kitchen, and dining hall. One gate in the iron railing let onto a tiny chapel, with an image of Our Lady of Charity, three benches, a corridor, and at its end the death cell. A second entry accessed the office of Captain Alfonso Zayas. "This way, Father, the captain is expecting you."

Nothing in either the physical appearance or the manners of the captain coincided with the archetype that one typically associated with a guerrilla, even much less the warden of a revolutionary prison. Least of all were his eyes, his gaze. I was told later that his behavior in the face of the enemy used to be wild, one of absolute bravery and courage; that at the battle of Santa Clara train station, the previous Christmas, he had acted in a way normally attributed to heroes, and that he was a man trusted by Che. That was not my initial impression. Rather, it was of someone who was more simply out of place than truly exceptional. He matched more closely the image of a young Catholic Action member in the parish of Puerto Padre, a modest young man whose wings had been clipped, not prone to speaking much and still less dissenting, with very sick eyes, deep-set in a pool of reddish water. A jailer with that appearance? One would say he resembled more an authentic sacristan.

"In Puerto Padre, a year ago, you [*tú*] would never have imagined this, right?" His membership of the JAC (Young Catholic Action) smoothed our way for the informal use of *tú*. "I don't know how you're feeling, but I'd be afraid to be in your position looking after that pack of wolves locked up there in the courtyard." "Well, yes and no, in December there were a lot more wolves than now, defeat has left them downhearted, they still haven't taken it all in. Happy? Bah, someone's got to do it. And you're planning to hear confession from all these people?" "Well, I don't think so, maybe no one, but fate has decreed that I'm your parish priest, I don't like it, but someone has to do it, even me, and here I am for anything they may need." "I think your job is more difficult and unpleasant than mine, Father, I wish you luck."

I went out into the courtyard and suddenly had the feeling that a transparent but rock- hard glass wall was arising between them and me, that it was moving alongside me, that we were staring at each other, listening to each another, but there was no communication. There is no doubt they could smell my train of thought. They realized I was on the other side, they didn't feel I was one of them, maybe they recalled the carrion-eating ravens the people likened to priests and saw me as the messenger of catastrophes. They were two steps away from me, why was I regarding and feeling them to be so distant? I went up to a small group that was talking in lively fashion. Suddenly there was silence as if they were blocks of impenetrable bluish limestone, their eyes fixed on me. "Good morning, I'm Father Javier, the parish priest of Casa Blanca, how are you?" Nobody answered, they challenged me with their stares. Nor could I think of anything to say to break the ice. "How do you think we feel? Content? Happy? Can't you grasp the idea that everyone is unhappy? You could have asked us anything else, we're not well, period."

There's always one who is different. He saw what had just happened and came to my rescue. He introduced himself, I don't remember his name; he attended some other church that I don't recall in Havana, and offered to serve as my guide. We struck up a conversation. I asked him how many of them there were. "I don't know exactly, eight hundred? Soon there will be a thousand of us if they keep on bringing more people in, we'll be sleeping on top of one another, we won't be able to move around in the courtyard, like sardines in a can." Two or three others joined us, like bodyguards. They took me to see the galleries, the vaulted tunnels in which they slept. I was struck by the number of occupied bunk beds. Were they sleeping now at this time? Would they be sleeping in turns? We walked to the back. There was an iron-barred window in the wall, about two meters thick maybe? It let in little light and ventilation for such long galleries, two scarcely-concealed lavatories and two showers on each side of the window. There were between eighty and one hundred men assigned to each gallery; they stank, naturally enough. At night it had to be horrible. I didn't even want to think about what it would be like if there was an outbreak of dysentery here. Good God! The dining hall was the same as any other cell, with tables and benches instead of bunkbeds. The kitchen, an oven, unbearable. The food was by now almost ready. I tried a bit of rice and red beans. It was not so bad, perhaps it lacked a little salt and oil. The pantry and provision of comestibles had been inherited from the previous regime.

They were living through some bad times, perhaps the worst in their lives. Prison threatens human beings to their core. The lack of freedom makes them sick, and, if they see that hope is fading, depression may strike them down and corrode their souls. When they believed their questions were being answered, they bombarded me with inquiries. They really wanted to know what was going on. What was being said on the streets, in the press, what was going to be done with them. "Is it true the trials are going to take place right here, in La Cabaña? Soon? When?" They took me by surprise. They didn't believe that I knew nothing. I would have to prepare myself before each visit in order to respond less ambiguously. But I'd also need to bring them more than just the latest news in order to alleviate their anxieties. I offered to serve as a contact with their families if they gave me their telephone numbers, to mail any letters they might have. I volunteered to bring them clothes, medicine, whatever; I'd deliver anything I was given for them. Just so long as it was legal. I shook hands with quite a lot of them—some hands said to me "I need you, help me," others said nothing. I left with a "see you tomorrow." It was midday; my stay had lasted two and a half hours.

I spent all afternoon digesting the visit. The buzzing of the courtyard remained in my ears, the nervous tension of the prisoners in my soul. The "we're not well" of the spokesman of the first group continued to slap me in the face for hours. I felt sorry for those men. A couple of weeks earlier they had been the ones in charge. Havana functioned according to their rules, and to the rhythm that they set. Now, on losing their freedom, they were wingless hawks, ugly and loathed, nobody was interested in what they thought or wanted. They knew and felt that the hatred of the people flowed over them from head to foot, like foul-smelling, sticky honey. They were gripped by fear and they had good reason to be. As a Christian and a priest, I had no other alternative than to turn to the charity I had learned in the Gospel. As a person who had, more or less close up in Spain, seen and experienced how those men operated, sometimes obeying orders and other times following the instincts of bloodthirsty wolves, I couldn't stop detesting the brutal and corrupt world they had created and defended. Given that, when the time came, they would be held to account and they would have to respond, "there's no use crying over spilled milk." But loving and detesting are not good bedfellows. Taming wolves, as did Saint Francis with the Gubbio one, smacks of legend; loving wolves seems like Good Friday. I was at the edge of a pit that spiraled down until one lost sight of bottom in the darkness of the chasm. A kind of electric shock ran down my spine and my mind was paralyzed, numb, lacking any response, incapable of listening to or asking questions. This was a huge mess.

I went back to the prison the following day. And the next day and the day after that. The looks of many wounded me like arrows in my heart. It was difficult to remain indifferent in the face of the indifference of others. That was the result, I thought, of superstitions and undereducated and ill-informed factions; I tried to ignore them. Those that approached me to chat were, more than anything else, seeking news about what was going on in the streets, what the press was saying, a glimmer or trace that could filter in a ray of light or hope for them. What awaited Cuba? How long would the revolutionary government last? What would follow it? What did I know?

The flood of errands I had feared that first day never materialized. Not from inside the prison out or the outside in. Maybe they didn't think of me as a safe errand boy. Maybe they didn't want a stranger getting too close to their private familial and matrimonial affairs. Something happened instead that left a lasting impact on me; something far removed from the tension and atmosphere that reigned in the prison. The owner of a fur store in Muralla Street came to where I lived in the San Francisco monastery in Aguiar Street, and spoke to me about a friend of his who was imprisoned in La Cabaña. He wanted me to pass along to him a casserole dish that contained a rabbit fricassee. "It's one of his favorite dishes and it'll help to cheer him up. I'm sure of it." I found the recipient in the courtyard, he had occupied a senior position in a national bank, and he received his friend's gift enthusiastically. Thereafter, every other day, one yes the other no, he feasted on three rabbits that I never sampled, but which gave off a five-star aroma. The banker didn't spend too many days in prison, and, thanks to his furrier friend in Muralla Street, the incarceration didn't get him down too much. It was just a nuisance. It wasn't the most rewarding charitable act I ever undertook.

The revolutionary justice's investigation and records office, the Auditory, had been set up two steps away from the green doors of the prison, under the command of Captain Miguel Angel Duque Estrada. From his desk, he saw me going in the direction of the prison every morning and returning at midday. "Father, come in, don't you want to hear the news?" I suspected he was doing this so that I would pass it on that afternoon or the next day in the courtyard. I filtered the information. It was fine for them to keep informed, but some news would have been an explosive for them and I wasn't going to be the one to light the fuse. "What's all this about your priestly role when all you do is dump on us this harsh information?" After a few days a certain amount of trust arose between the priest and the revolutionary shyster, who had been educated at a religious school: "Father, how are you today?" We were both out of our element, treading on shifting sand, this wasn't our thing—that's how I saw it.

"The first bomb will drop this month and many more will fall in a row during the ones that follow. It's going to be tough, Father, the prison will be brought to a fever pitch, very difficult." "Do you think Che would be against my trying to organize among the prisoners a kind of missionary campaign?" "What would that be?" "Hmm, well I'll speak with Father Chaurrondo, from the Vincentians, let's see if he'll lend me a couple of missionaries and a couple of nuns from the Charity so that they can come next week to speak to them about God or whatever they want. The thing is, if they're going to die, they should have the opportunity to leave having repented and been pardoned." "And why don't you do it, as they already know you?" "For exactly the same reason, because they've figured me out and they know me. Or they think they know me."

"'Opium' for those on their way to death? So they go silently, submissively, obediently, so we don't have to drag them along all tied up, whipping them as we go? They don't deserve it, it wasn't their own style, but give it a go, see what happens." That's how Che replied.

Green is the star of hope,
the sign of life.
Who was that dreadful person
who ordered the prison doors
to be painted green?
My God! And how green!
The rawest, most garish and insolent
wild green
ripping out the guts
of the forest,
green insult, a taunting
green belly laugh,
crackling green flame:
leave your hopes behind here
those of you who come destined
to crack under my arms.
Olive green militiamen
guard the main doors.
Not even a trace of hope,
they have been told,

must cross these bars.
We'll build a gallows
in the center of the courtyard
and around the neck a noose we'll tie
to hopes and dreams.
Here is the kingdom of death!
How sick, my God, the mind
of someone prepared to paint in green
the prison doors.

# 5

I went to La Merced Church, that of the Vincentians, in Cuba Street, Old Havana, and asked to speak with Father Hilario Chaurrondo. He was known well throughout the island for his missionary work, above all in inland parishes. I didn't know whether he was actually in Cuba and at home in Havana, or if he was interested seeing me, or could in fact do so. "Let's see who appears, I'm not leaving until I speak with someone. Father Obanos? Good." I explained my plan to him. "And I want this for tomorrow, it has to be straightaway, without leaving room for a change in the direction of the wind, without losing time, above all before the trials begin and the courtyard is covered in hot coals so that no Christian could set foot there. Publicity? Pave the way? No way, it's better to take them by surprise, help is assured, attending there to anyone, it's not up to us. What's more I'm convinced the nuns will be the best publicists, the condemned will listen to them much more than to us preachers. Topics? You're the experts, right? Death, justice, hell, heaven, grace and sin, the commandments, the Prodigal Son, repentance. Talk about anything except getting embroiled in the ideas being launched here, a quick word about the revolution and that's it. That's how things are, yes sir." "And why don't you help us?" "Because I don't want to, because I can't, because my time to act will come and I'll have no one to assist me."

The mission was held. For four days, morning and afternoon, two sisters of Mercy and two Vincentian fathers circulated among them and spoke completely freely, attempting to impart the Christian message of salvation to the inmates. A significant group surrounded the sermonizing preacher attentively. Many, I'd say most, assumed postures and masks of indifference or disinterest. They shuffled here and there, and moved to the other side of the courtyard, alone, heads down, as if it had nothing to do with them, but still soaking up the sermon from afar. A few withdrew to the very back of the galleries to play *briscola*, *tute*, or chess, to smoke and to chat. There was no outcry or demonstration of disapproval on the part of anyone. During the final act, I myself said Mass and administered between twenty-five and thirty communions. During the mission, one inmate asked me to fix his marriage, bless it, and I did so, without the least bit of regret. A friend of the unlucky guy himself and Captain Alfonso Zayas acted as witnesses.

Was the mission worth it? Was it the most appropriate thing to do at that particular moment? Were we wasting our time? Nobody can say for sure. Sometimes mystery grabs us by the hand and leads us away, one sees better in the shade than in the light, one hears more amid noise than in silence, the word takes the form of a living presence. There are rainstorms that lead to flooding and inundation, and those that soak into and saturate the landscape, for which the latter is thankful. I'll leave it at that. There were comments and jokes, not too many and not too crude, on the role of prominent rebel army officials in La Cabaña. At certain times seeking to get closer to God and asking for his forgiveness, speaking about death and divine justice, seemed in bad taste to me, knowing what was about to happen within that walled enclosure. It would be like mentioning the noose in the hangman's home. Who knows, however, whether it was precisely in that "calling a spade a spade" that many found the means with which to develop greater courage, and, illumined, to head toward their great silence, there, right around the corner.

The courtyard was boiling. It was a cauldron of passion, of frustration, of bitterness, of resentment, of worry, of jealousy, of fear—all bubbling over. I took part in the spectacle, I wanted to participate, to hold out my hand, pour water on the fire, to advise. They were falling before one's very eyes, a forest of decapitated giants who, before, machine gun in hand, exerted power, force, cruelty, and now slipping into the shadows, nobodies at the mercy of the old enemy, filled with the feeling of being unloved, of not deserving to be loved. The god they believed themselves to be was being smashed to pieces. What could I do for them? Very little. They had to get closer to the edge, see themselves hanging over the abyss, then they would surely relent and allow themselves to be helped. It was a painful metamorphosis toward a change of attitude, a new dimension, the desire to have been someone else, a vision of the new man, a farewell to being in which one ceases to be a man of this earth. What was I going to do in the courtyard if I too was sick? The same as them, I imagine.

I was involved in something during one of the days that followed the mission that still shocks and astonishes me; it's difficult to accept that I did it. It was fine in the end, no one found out, but it could have involved several people in a fatal outcome. I went over to greet a prisoner and he asked me to step to one side. His manners were good, not arrogant at all, and with a slight touch of nerves. He presented himself as someone who had for some years commanded the national police barracks in Santiago de las Vegas until last New Year's Day. I didn't know him, nor had I heard anything about him during the four years I had lived in the Franciscan seminary in the same municipality, on the outskirts of his town. He assured me he could have gone into hiding before they came to arrest him, but that he didn't do so because he had never been involved in any bloody events, and he didn't think he would be unduly singled out. "It just so happens, Father, that my mom is sick and we're afraid she's going to die without me being able to see her. The only way out I can think of is for you to intervene on my behalf. You could ask for a day-pass, they might give it me and authorize you to take me to my mom's house." "Young man, you're not right in the head. How can you think such nonsense? I'll go and see your mom, and I'll pass on whatever you give me. I'll bring you whatever she gives me, but how could I take you to see her? What if they were to arrest us? What if you were to escape from me?"

The following morning, however, I sat down at Captain Alfonso's desk. "Alfonso, I need you to do me a big favor, look, it's about a family I knew," that wasn't true, "when I taught at the Santiago de las Vegas seminary. I can assure you that this will remain confidential—that not even my left hand will find out what the right is doing. And, of course, you have the word of a friend that I will turn myself in to revolutionary justice if, by that afternoon, I'm not here in your office handing over the prisoner. Let me take him home so his mother can see him before God takes her." Alfonso looked at me for a long time, with his childlike sick eyes, pursing his lips, incredulously. I put up with his stare. "Do you realize what you're asking me Father Javier?" "Yes, of course I do." "Do you insist?" "I insist." "Wait a moment, stay right here and don't talk to anyone."

After a while the two of them showed up, the former police-officer prisoner in his civilian clothes. "You realize that if you don't come back this afternoon with the Father to this very spot where we are right now, he," pointing at me with his finger, "will almost certainly be tried and possibly executed? Remember you're not carrying any papers, behave naturally, pray along the way—until the afternoon." During that time I had access to a car for my personal use. So we didn't need to talk to anyone on leaving the camp, where I was already very well known, nor along the way either, until I dropped him off at the door of a house where he said his mother lived. "I'll come and collect you at four o´clock sharp, I hope your family is well. Say hello to your mom from me."

I went to the seminary to spend the day there. On the outskirts of town, three kilometers away, on the road to Managua, in the country. I was as antsy as a dog shaking off fleas, unable to string together four sentences, without any appetite, looking at my watch every two minutes, chain smoking like a truck driver. "But Javier, what's up with you? You're unrecognizable. Do you not feel well?" Such a long day, in the middle of a field, without any birds, any flowers, any breeze, any sky, with dribs and drabs of oxygen. At four o'clock sharp he was waiting for me, seated outside the house with his mom. I hugged them. I breathed a deep sigh of relief. An hour later I handed him in at the prison office and I understood, relishing the feeling, what it must be like to be reborn.

Every morning, Duque Estrada's Auditory was a crowd of people coming and going. "What are you doing with such a procession of women and men?" They were the witnesses who would testify before the courts. Witnesses uttering in sworn declarations their recollections of the night the police took their father, brother, or son away, never to be seen alive again. Some of them were not about individual deaths, but rather the night an army patrol entered the village, razed everything to the ground, leaving only smoking ruins, and then the afternoon that . . . Whosoever could not remember details or express them in words was provided these prompts, either the concepts or set phrases. That's where I first met Carbó Serviá's mother—what a picture of an honorable matron, snow-white hair, an elegant demeanor, sad eyes, forced to recall and ready to forgive and forget. That's where I met a group of *guajiros* (country bumpkins) from the Sierra Maestra, all of them fish out of water, who, with great difficulty, had been led to respond to the investigators, without realizing what was going on, or what was happening to them.

The time had come, Duque Estrada told me one afternoon. "We'll start tomorrow, make a note of the date, January 28, and be sure to get to the courtyard early. It'll be worth it." In effect, once the news was made public, the courtyard sizzled, as tempers began to boil. That afternoon, Jesús Sosa Blanco, Pedro Morejón, and Luis Ricardo Grao, three high-ranking officials in Batista's army, would be tried for events that had taken place in the Sierra Maestra. The trial would take place in the recently constructed and inaugurated Palacio de los Deportes, at the exit toward Rancho Boyeros, just beyond the illuminated fountain, at the beginning of Santa Catalina Avenue. There was free entry and everyone was invited to attend; the event would also be transmitted on TV.

I did indeed encounter a red-hot courtyard. Crackles of raised voices could be heard on all sides, continuously, expressing multiple points of view, conjectures, accusations, threats. "They want to make us disappear, we have the right to be represented by the lawyers of our choice, they're motherless murderers and we should have eliminated them when we had the chance." Shouts bounced off the walls and disappeared into the clear blue sky. The courtyard emitted a kind of twisted negative energy that made it difficult to breathe. There were few words as I passed by them, rather cold steely looks, clenched fists, short sharp movements, like lightning bolts striking trees.

I was taken to a group in which Sosa Blanco was in the middle. Up until that moment, I hadn't sketched his features in the notebook of my memory. I now observed that he was one of those whose face could be defined and recorded in four strokes. Thin, strong, a jet black beard, the eyes of a nice guy—yes, yes. Fidel had already condemned him, the court would condemn him once again, and yet he had the eyes of a nice guy, sunken in the shadow of abundant black foliage eyebrows. On seeing me, without coming over, but conscious of the fact I was listening, he said—and I don't know if he repeated it—that he was going to be thrown to the lions that afternoon, like the Christians in Rome. Had he seen, I wondered, or been told about the movie *Quo Vadis*? I came very, very close to clarifying with him the similarities and differences between what had happened in Rome nineteen hundred years previously and what was happening in Havana today. At the right moment, I kept my mouth shut and let him repeat over and over again his impotence, his bitterness. I approached him. We looked at each other intensely. That face had in a short time become for me very close, friendly, familiar. At that moment I saw it sullen, distant, hostile. I put my hand on his shoulder. "I don't know if it will make any difference, but I'll be there this afternoon. I promise you."

I'd like, Father,
to put my past in order
before taking the step,
to do it in time.
That's fine.
Just realize that now
what's important is what's comving,
not what's already been.
Give me your hands,
let's form a hollow
closed off at the sides.
Empty into there however much you wanted to
put in order.
When your time comes to meet the time of
God,
which is time unlike ours
because it is eternal,
open your hands and you'll see that they are
clean.
They are clean on coming into contact with the
Light

from which all lights are born,
on encountering the Life
from which all lives flow
with its own space and time,
on meeting God
in whom all of us have been forever,
from which all man's paths
leave and return.
Those paths we've traveled
without realizing where they started
or what their destination was.
And it won't be necessary to remember
the time we wasted
nor forget we existed.
In God
everything is Light
and everything is Life.

# 6

When I went along to his office in the morning, I had asked Captain Duque Estrada for permission to sit next to him during the trial. I had never attended legal proceedings, and, without any guidance, without questions and answers, and without commentary, I would most likely miss half of what was going on and only half understand the other half. I didn't want that to happen.

Jesús Sosa Blanco, like Pedro Morejón and Luis Ricardo Grao, had been sentenced to death a month before. This happened in the main square of Santiago de Cuba, in the early morning of January 2, in the middle of a pseudo-sacramental rite that the Revolution had established five (or was it six?) hours earlier: the interminable nocturnal discourse, filled with the infallible assertions of the supreme leader. A rite that remained unshakeable for years until Fidel aged and started to run out of breath. That first day, without trials, without judges, or prosecuting attorneys, or defense lawyers, or witnesses, Fidel Castro Ruz sentenced to death and promised before the people of Cuba, and before the world, that Jesús Sosa Blanco, Pedro Morejón, and Luis Ricardo Grao would be executed. *Lider maximus dixit.*

Fidel Castro ordered the organization of, and then led, the lengthiest and longest-lasting victory parade in the history of Cuba, the Americas, and, I think, the world. It was a journey from Santiago de Cuba to Havana lasting ten days. By day, by night, without any schedules, without pre-established programs, without any hurry, without rest. Cuba turned out along the main highway to witness it pass by, to listen to it with reverential fervor, the souls on their knees, as if before an oracle, a prophet, a messiah. And, in every speech, Fidel ratified the dictated sentence dictated in the first one.

With the triumphal entrance of Castro and his cohort into the Columbia military camp, and the message he aimed *urbi et orbi*, it was established that Cuba had embraced as its own the vision of a new world and of history, and was premiering a new way of life: the Revolution. It was done without any protocol, without any transition or transfer of powers, without any sort of prior consultation, through the sole force of *faits accomplis*. He did not claim God as his witness or place his hand on the bible or the constitution. He did not swear on anything or promise allegiance to anything or anyone.

He demanded everyone's submission before the laws emanating from the revolution. And he guaranteed that all of its enemies would be wiped out. He assured everyone that, soon, Cuba and the world would be witness to a demonstration of how they, the just, would judge and punish bloody murderers like Sosa Blanco, Morejón, and Grao.

Excesses had already been committed during the first few days, outbursts incapable of constraining the euphoria of triumph, deplorable. Not even in the bloodiest text of revolutionary practices could one find anything like the establishment of a people's court, presenting it with several dozen (around seventy) subjects deserving of the maximum sentence, cross-examining them individually, one by one, applying legal criteria to their cases, judging them, sentencing them, and executing them. And all that between mid-afternoon and midnight during one twenty-four-hour day. It had happened. Everyone knew that it took place in Santiago de Cuba, capital of the province of Oriente, and specifically on the orders of Raúl Castro, Fidel's brother. The world's press had shown what would become emblematic, that man draped in an overcoat and collapsed against an improvised execution wall, in Caibarién, Las Villas, if I'm not mistaken, while his hat flew in the air. They were false, distorted images—understandable errors amid all the confusion of triumph—that were now going to be replaced by the true picture of true revolutionary justice. In order to see that I headed to the Palacio de los Deportes (Sports Palace) during the early afternoon of January 28, 1959.

I half-close my eyes and it seems as if I'm watching a rush of people toward the sports center in Santa Catalina and the road to Boyeros, to half-fill its total seating capacity, although at the same time threatening to explode on account of all the shouting. They expected more people, a lot more people. They also expected more of a show. Perhaps—and even without any perhaps—if they had announced executions at 5 o'clock in the afternoon, waves of women and men, children, young people, adults, and old folk, all of them treading on each other in an effort to get in, would have crushed all access to the site. But Fidel had already judged them, the people must have thought, what could this trial have offered that was anything new or eye-catching? Indeed, as a show, it was quite tedious, slow, and boring. When night fell, and on seeing that the function of the theater was being dragged out without any signs of improvement, so began the homeward march of the onlookers.

The court had been set up, with a two-hour delay, at around five in the afternoon. It was constituted by three judges, three rebel army officers who were acting as judges. None of them was a professional judge, I don't know if they were lawyers or legal experts, I don't think so. I seem to recall that Raúl Chibás and Sorí Marín were two of the three, but I'm not very sure. I don't remember much about the prosecuting attorney, apart from his passion and frequent irate outbursts. It wasn't, in any case, De la Fuente, who weeks later had to make do in La Cabaña with the deserved nickname of "El Chacal" (The jackal) for his ferocity. It was the defense attorney, Lawyer D'Acosta, an official of the prerevolutionary navy and appointed for the occasion, who stole the show that night. He was the court-appointed lawyer for this trial because the accused could not defend themselves, nor had they been given the opportunity to hire the services of anyone else, in the event that there was anyone else in Cuba at that moment. Who would have been bold enough to enter the fray and defend monsters so angrily condemned over and over again by Fidel Castro?

Lawyer D'Acosta was a meteorite of blinding light in that night of revolutionary justice. If anyone had been capable of imagining and predicting the devastating role that he was going to play in that revolutionary justice, which was crowed about and dressed up so thoroughly, they would not have turned to him. Not in their wildest dreams. He was responsible for the demonstration to the outside world that the show was compromised, ending in a stampede and a headlong rush to justice; like trying to say a dawn rosary in the midst of a lighting storm and torrential rain. It was the first and last trial in front of the television cameras and with unrestricted public access. It was the first and last performance by Lawyer D'Acosta.

The three accused, already condemned by the supreme leader, were seated opposite the three judges. Surrounding all of them was a "rebel" squad in the attire and trinkets that previously served to distinguish them in their so-called war in the Sierra Maestra, and that now served them within the folklore of victory—resolute, armed, bayonets fixed. Later, already dragging on into a night measured by the clock and the ridiculousness and desperation, I was assured that, according to initial calculations, the evening and night would be divided as follows: two hours to question each of the accused and their witnesses, two more for the final arguments of the prosecuting attorney and the defense lawyer, one for deliberations behind closed doors, one more for reading out the sentence in the presence of the Fidel-Raúl-Camilo-Che quartet, and then the typical little speech by Fidel, one hour to make up for any delays, and, at daybreak, possibly in La Cabaña, the executions.

They began with the most notorious defendant, with Jesús Sosa Blanco. The president of the court spoke slowly, solemnly, without gesticulating, accentuating each word in the emptiness of the silence. "Will the accused stand up. This revolutionary court will judge you for the mass murder you ordered in the villages of humble farmers located in the foothills of the Sierra Maestra, events that occurred in the month of October 1957—the prosecuting attorney has the floor."

From my seat halfway up the amphitheater, in the least crowded area among all the people gathered, my eyes sought out Captain Duque Estrada. I didn't see him anywhere. He should have arrived; he should have been there. The prosecutor began to get carried away in describing the events. I tried to focus my attention.

According to him, "on October 12, 1957, Colonel Jesús Sosa Blanco in Batista's army was commanding a battalion of soldiers sent out to locate and eliminate a group of guerrillas that had been spotted by a military plane in the vicinity of the village of Quebrada Alta. By mid-afternoon, the search had proved futile and he ordered the troops to make camp and rest for the night while he went around the small wooden palm-leaved houses of the peasants to investigate where the rebels were hiding—where they had hidden them. After seeing the villagers refusing to offer any information"—how could they if they hadn't seen any movements on the part of the rebel militiamen?—"the accused there present threatened to do away with anyone refusing to hand over the enemy on the grounds of aiding and abetting them. When night fell, bursts of gunfire were heard around the troops' camp, a crude set up that served as the pretext for the soldiers to respond by bombing the village with incendiary devices. It was a night of indiscriminate killing in which men, women, old people, and children died. Here among us are the survivors that were able to flee into the night and hide. We will hear from their own lips the awful testimonies of how they saw their families and neighbors die, like animals, at the hands of the henchmen of this subhuman before our very eyes here."

When the prosecutor sat down after calling for the death penalty for the accused, something unreal floated around in my head for a few minutes. Was this a case of a man who, for whatever reason, went crazy and ordered the killing of anything that moved, human or animal, or a legend that had been cultivated in which evil took the form of a fiery sword or a ball of fire in the name of a rational being roaming the villages of the Sierra Madre night after night after night taking innocent lives? "Is what I am hearing fiction or reality?" I asked myself, head in hands.

Lawyer D'Acosta was very brief. He stated that he knew nothing of the case. "I have just read copies of the witnesses' sworn statements, I don't know my defendant's version, I haven't spoken to him, I have to question the witnesses separately one-by-one and question the accused in order to build up a more complete and, who knows, more accurate picture of what happened in Quebrada Alta on the night of October 12, 1957."

When the first witness was called up to testify, I saw that a group of officials, with Miguel Angel Duque Estrada at their head, was taking their places in the stands; not in the first rows, but an area relatively close to the tables and chairs of the judges, secretaries, officials, and the rest of the court's components. Without thinking twice, I stood up and made my way toward them.

A routine greeting. "How do you see all this?" Him: "Nothing new, it will get interesting now and we'll hear the rattling of machine guns and rifles." I was shocked, and just wanted it all to end there and then, regretting having come. Well, no, I had to come, I promised the prisoners that I would be there, but I was truly shocked and quite disgusted.

It was the most surreal and cruelest part of the trial, as well as being the longest and most tedious. At first I felt curiosity. This turned into surprise and astonishment. It ended up being disgust and repugnance. Something similar to what must happen to an overly sensitive person on witnessing the entrance of a cart in which some circuses show off human beings who have had the misfortune to come into this world deformed, with congenital defects that disfigure them, and which produces nausea among some, compassion in others, and hilarity for others still.

The witnesses brought in from the Sierra Maestra were, without any doubt, knowledgeable about life and its mysteries, illiterate, but blessed with intelligence, inner nobility, skills and qualities to communicate among themselves. They were able to relate to one another as well as any university professor or the most eminent surgeon. Placed before the spotlights of the stage and the television lights, however, in the buzzing of voices, shouts, and whistles of people they could not see but felt pressuring them, like a threatening thunderous sky, in the face of the irksome banter of the prosecuting attorney and his demands: "answer," "explain," "turn toward the court," "clarify," "louder," "once again," "it appears that you don't understand," and so forth—those poor *guajiros* from the mountains felt stunned, blinded, cornered, crushed. In another environment, another kind of communication, they could have handled it. But without so many lights, so much shouting, with the respect their situation demanded. They couldn't function in this subculture of noises, threats, and urgencies into which they had just been thrust.

You felt sorry for them. They acted like a herd of timid cows fleeing a pack of wild dogs biting at their legs and that end up drowning in a lake. They were used to influence the trial and ended up drowning in the same lake. In the ensuing mess, created in large measure by Lawyer D'Acosta, he was the only one to gain any benefit from it. The more he harassed the witnesses with his questions and insistences, the more they became confused, the more they doubted, the more they made no sense, the more they got lost in contradictions. And the truth and the heralded evidence retreated further away than ever.

The process continued and a new witness was presented. "Look at the court and answer my questions: name, age, civil status, residence, work or profession." Next to me, Duque Estrada was taking deep breaths, gently stroking his beard. "Let's see if this guy remembers the morning rehearsal and doesn't forget or make a fool of himself." He didn't say it out loud, but I'm sure inside his head he was adding: "nor make a fool out of us." Of course there had been a rehearsal. One by one. Over and over again. But they weren't being taught to grow corn or *yautias*, but instead to demonstrate their legitimacy amid a barrage of what, for them, were abstract questions, some active, others passive, many in complex periphrases, in language they were barely able to understand. In short, at this stage of the game, the trial was already a derailed train. Who knows whether, under different conditions, with the TV cameras switched off and the press, both homegrown and foreign, absent, the judges would have been able to decide that the allegations had been proven beyond a doubt and there was no need to hear any more testimonies. "They are guilty, we sentence them to death, the trial is over, the session is adjourned, turn off the lights, let's go."

At around two in the morning the court decreed a recess and withdrew to deliberate. The prosecutor left from behind the judges. The defense lawyer did not move from his table. A few minutes later, Duque Estrada was summoned. When he returned a half hour later, I wouldn't say it was difficult to recognize him, but he had definitely changed, he was someone else. Very serious, very unsettled. He came straight toward me to see if I could go to La Cabaña right then and there; if I had transportation? I asked him if they were going to execute Sosa Blanco, and he replied that he didn't know, that I should wait for them in the office of Alfonso Zayas.

On leaving the coliseum I looked one last time at the improvised court's stage. The amphitheater lights had been turned off, but the focal lights were still on. The lawyer remained seated at his table, his beard resting on his right hand. The three defendants also remained seated, still. A couple of steps away were the guards—olive green, long guns. Silence. Mystery. And now what?

I don't know how that gala night of revolutionary justice ended in the Sports Palace on Santa Catalina Avenue. Among the several versions I heard later, the most plausible one attributed the suspending of the trial to the highest people in the revolutionary hierarchy, Che, Camilo, Raúl, and Fidel, who had followed on television the details of the setback. I also heard it said that the decision was not unanimous, that someone had recommended that, although the trial had been suspended, Sosa Blanco should be executed that very night.

Good morning, Lord God.
From the "gallery of death,"
in La Cabaña.
I don't know you, we don't know each other.
They baptized me,
but they spoke to me
about you.
Let me introduce myself.
I'm X.X.
No one is interested in my name.
If you are what I've heard you are,
you must know it. I'll carry on.
They brought me here a week ago.
A dark, dirty, and narrow place,
In which I don't know how, but I'm seeing it,
past lights are gradually being switched off,
and a white light, a very white light, is
beginning
to be turned on inside me,
inside my soul.

I always thought that life
was meant to be lived and that living it
meant cutting off the best piece
to the trio "rum, women, and song."
I took up arms in order to honor the memory
of grandad and pop,
not because of any special calling.
I knew that things both inside and outside the
barracks
were not so good, worse than good.
And what could I do about it?

It's true that on more than one occasion
I lost control,
but I don't think I ever ended up
killing anyone,
not intentionally at least.
But it wasn't that, Lord God,
that I wanted to speak to you about.
Every night we are visited by
a young priest.
We chat, we smoke, he replies to
the questions we ask him,
not about everything, from what I see,
he hides what he thinks may bother us,
we even tell stories and have a laugh.
All of a sudden he speaks about You,
about Jesus, about the Gospel,
and he explains the words of the Lord's Prayer,
about your love, your will, your kingdom.

Then he gets us to say the rosary.
I don't know how to say it,
I move my lips
as if I were praying,
and I let my soul be struck
when over and over again,
in a bell metal voice,
my friend repeats over and
over again,
"now and at the time of our death."

Without realizing it, I'm beginning to
understand
what it means to walk toward the shore
of this life
and I'm beginning to understand
that I need a bridge to take me to the
shore of the other life.
Lord, is it true
that you'll be waiting there?
In that event, would you help me
to raise the bridge,
I from my side and you from your side?
I hope so.
Holy Father: in the "gallery of death,"
in La Cabaña,
we need you, we call on you, we love you.
Yours, X. X.

# 7

Havana slept swathed in silence and in a discrete yellowish light, with scarcely any display of neon. I crossed it from south to north, knowing where I was heading and wishing that the way there were longer, much longer, as distant as the last shaded part of the nocturnal sky, that I would never reach my final destination. Consumed by preoccupations, wanting to get lost, and never ever to arrive. I was obsessed with one question: "what do I say to Sosa Blanco when we find ourselves alone?" What does one say on such occasions? What would Father Melo say to him? The man who every day experienced this trance of presenting a moribund man to his "sister," the lady of death who was coming for him?" I arrived at La Cabaña and the question kept on tormenting me. "What do I tell him? What?"

Shortly afterward the handcuffed prisoners, the officials, and some soldiers arrived. They went through the green gate in total silence. The courtyard was empty, spotlights half languid on a post, the galleries closed, darkness, some gray ghosts peering out from behind the bars. Captain Alfonso Zayas took charge of the group. He guided us into the chapel by the door leading out directly to the gate and entered a narrow corridor, its walls bare, doors closed on both sides. At the end, turning left, there was another short corridor, four dark cells along its sides, with bars at their front, a single light bulb on the ceiling, a dark murky light, and at the rear a small window in the wall beyond which one perceived the night.

He stopped at the first cell on the right. He took Luis Ricardo Grao by the arm, removed his handcuffs, ushered him into the cell, closed the door, bolted it shut, and padlocked it. He repeated the same procedures in the first cell to left and Pedro Morejón was locked up. After two steps toward the second cell on the right-hand side., he took the handcuffs off Jesús Sosa Blanco who went in without having been told to do so. Captain Zayas turned toward me: "Are you going in?" "Yes." The door remained open behind us.

We looked at each other and, without saying a word, spontaneously and clumsily we embraced one another. Intensely. Extendedly. Silently. I felt his strong palpations. He must have felt mine. "They're going to execute me," he said after a while. "I don't think so, the trial isn't over yet, they can't execute you," I answered. "But let's speak about something else. Do you know how to pray?" "Yes." "Then we're going to pray together, slowly, we're in no hurry, I'll start and you follow me . . . Our Father, who art in heaven . . . hallowed be thy name . . . thy kingdom come . . . thy will be done . . . on earth as it is in heaven . . . give us this day our daily bread . . . and forgive us our trespasses . . . as we forgive those who trespass against us . . . and lead us not into temptation . . . but deliver us from evil."

The Lord's Prayer was followed by Ave Maria, Lord Jesus Christ, and the Salve Regina. "Again," he requested when we had finished. We repeated these several times. No words we could ever have said would have been enough, no questions, no comments. Praying and the clumsy embrace said a lot more. I don't know how long we remained like that. It must have been a long time. Suddenly, I saw a soft pale light, the daybreak of January 29. It started to feel its way in tentatively through the window in the corridor, almost as if afraid. I was nudged in the back. I looked up and saw a photographer positioning himself to capture the scene with his camera. He took a few shots. For a few instants, the flash revealed the squalor of the place, the murkiness, the emptiness, the starkness of the dirty walls.

"Father, as if you were giving a blessing," the photographer prompted. I looked at Sosa Blanco with a "what do you think?" expression. He nodded assent. I raised my hand to make the sign of the cross on his face. The photographer captured the moment on film. Later, on many occasions, I have thought that I should have put a stop to that photographic session. There are moments that should be respected, they belong exclusively to the people who experience them. The publishing, in the pages of the *Diario de la Marina* the following day, of pictures of Jesús Sosa Blanco and Father Javier embracing one another and praying and imparting blessings, walking toward death like two good Christians, submitting to God's will, it was all in bad taste, unseemly, dishonest. I have regretted those photos a thousand times and never wanted to possess them. Che, I know from his own lips, rejoiced when he read the newspaper report. He didn't tell me why.

Captain Zayas called me over. "I've just been informed that there will be no executions for the moment." I went back and told Sosa Blanco. "Try and sleep a bit. I'll come back at noon." I left very sadly. I didn't go back to my monastery in Old Havana or my Casa Blanca parish. I walked up to the wall. I sat down and looked out at the ocean over which the day was breaking. My heart felt like when your hands or legs go numb because of insufficient blood flow. My mind was totally empty.

Guardroom, dungeon, dark cell, vault. All that and much more. The dark, dirty cells into which the three condemned men were placed that early morning, awaiting their sentence from without, were baptized "the gallery of death" that afternoon. It lacked any adornments to expand on that or tone it down. Simply "the gallery of death," because it would detain prisoners awaiting their appearance before the courts constituted in La Cabaña fort. They would be judged and then made prisoners on death row. It was there they would live out their final days. There they would discover feelings and experience new horizons of life and of death. The fifty-five men whose death sentences were ratified and who were executed by firing squad between the months of February and May 1959 all left there to walk to the execution wall.

The gallery of death could house twelve people in its four cells, three in each under subhuman conditions. Without a table or chairs, without any bunk beds or mats, without a water source, without a latrine, without any receptacle in which to void.. It served them as a dwelling at the mid-point of the last seven days of their lives. There were days and nights in which there were more than twenty people in the four cells crowded together. They were herded into an adjacent bathroom twice a day. They were offered no medical services; no one was examined inside the cell or removed from it for health reasons. Once in "the gallery of death," they could easily have envied pigs in their pigsties.

As I promised them when I said goodbye, I came back at noon. I had made several decisions and I was keen for them to understand me clearly right from the outset. My greetings and exchanges of "how are you?" "did they bring you anything to eat?" "have you been able to get any sleep?" "do your families know the latest about you?" and "do you need anything I can get for you?" were expressed without any difficulty. I believe an atmosphere of familiar sounds and friends was established; that's what I thought. I felt they were more comforted than when they were walking around in the confused swarm of the courtyard. To be sure, tragedy stalked these men, felt, certainly, at least by those not made of stone.

"If you want and ask me, I will come up here every day, even several times a day, in the morning, afternoon, at night. Just let me know. We can speak about anything with two exceptions—politics and why you are all here. If you want to tell me in private, we'll see, but I'm not interested. If for the reason that I'm a priest anyone thinks that I'd like to hear your confession, you're completely mistaken. What's more, I'm not thinking of suggesting that you confess to me. If anyone is thinking of doing so, tell me and I'll tell you how to go about it, I'll look for someone to come and hear it. I don't think they'll let me bring any newspapers in with me, but I'll read them before coming up here if you want to know what's going on outside, in the streets, in the ballparks, in the world. Anyone who wants to write to his family or whomever or wants me to speak to them, please consider me entirely at your disposal. Above all, we don't know each other, but I want to be your friend—you can trust me."

It would have taken a lot for me to believe this if I were listening to it myself. Where did this all come from; just yesterday I wouldn't even have thought of speaking like this. Something had stirred in my very being because I swear that I was sincere, that I really felt what I was saying.

I had also made another decision, but I didn't say anything to them regarding it. They were there because they were going to be executed, because in all certainty the only way they were going to get out of that dungeon alive would be over the wall; both they and I knew that without anyone saying a word. But I refrained from speaking to them about death; of death as a consequence of man's sin. Above all, I avoided speaking about it as a door to an eternity of condemnation and suffering if one's evil sins were not erased beforehand through the absolution given by a priest. Nor was it talking to them about what was coming after death—who knows what's coming? To a group of people meeting in "spiritual exercises," for example, one can remind them that we live exposed to death and the mystery that surrounds it, and warn them that they have to assume that inevitably and live prepared for it. But not in the "gallery of death," not me. The topic would come up, I was sure. But why call attention to it? And I could barely manage to explain it. Two feelings clashed inside of me. I acknowledged that nothing in life is so serious, so important, or so dramatic as death. Likewise, I acknowledged that, when we preached about death it was the product of our imagination and fear, given that in reality we knew nothing about what happens during and after the event.

Nor did I think about talking to them about God on my own account. I was hoping that they would approach me about what was to be done. But it wouldn't be the God of the Sinai, jealous and demanding, He who judges and punishes, the arbitrator God, the accountant God, the concierge God, but instead He who seeks and waits and pardons, the "good shepherd." I'd speak to them about Christ, who had to listen to shouts of "crucify him, crucify him!" and was condemned to death and died on the cross, forgiven. But when the time was right. I wouldn't pester them. God, like death, would come in due time, it would do so by chance. I didn't have the slightest doubt that a speechless God would speak to them wordlessly much better than I could communicate about Him with my words.

That same night Jesús Sosa Blanco made the most of a lull in the conversation to ask me if we could pray. The prayers the night before had calmed him down a lot, they had made him feel much better. He asked me, moreover, to bring a book or pamphlet with prayers. At home, in his childhood, his mother had taught him to pray. When he left there as a young man to look for work and found it at a barracks, he had forgotten all about the prayers. Right now, his wife and daughters were good Catholics and did pray at home, although he didn't join in. He didn't whisper this into my ear. Everyone heard him, his companions and the militiamen guarding them. Luis Ricardo Grao, a former student of the Marist Brothers in Cienfuegos, suggested we say the rosary. Pedro Morejón agreed. "Whatever you prefer, I don't mind." That's how, on their initiative, saying the rosary every night was established in the "gallery of death." As a goodbye to the day, as a prelude to sleep, as contact with the beyond—with God. Many nights, once the rosary had ended, they asked me questions seeking to clarify their doubts or acquire more information or simply talk about God, about religion.

The gallery was calm for several days. We got used to its half-light, to the lugubrious icy emissions from its walls and dirty floor, to the thousand limitations. The assiduous mid-afternoon presence of Amelia, Sosa Blanco's wife, and their two adolescent daughters added a note of sweetness and light. Marcial, a militiaman assigned to guarding the prison, declared himself their protector, he waited for them and no one dared to bother them. It was moving to see Sosa Blanco put his rough hands through the bars to touch the faces of "my little girls," while his face and buffalo-like hair were transformed into a meadow of tenderness. I interrupted without wanting to a brief conversation between Jesús and his wife. "Amelia, I'd like you to do me a favor. Do you remember the shoes I bought for the New Year's Eve party but never got to wear? I'd like you to bring them, but without the girls realizing." "Why do you want them if you've never even bothered to wear the shoes you have since you've been here, you're always barefoot?" "I'm going to wear them the night they're going to execute me."

Amelia asked if she could speak to me alone, just she and I. "I know that you've told them that you're not interested in why they are there. I can imagine what your reasons are and I respect that. But I do want you to know that my husband is not the monster they say he is." She told me that her husband wasn't even a week in the Sierra. A day after arriving he had to take charge of some troops who were going to take up position on a mountain when they were surprised and ambushed by the guerrillas and they lost several men. In their pursuit of the rebels, who hid in a small village, and when they didn't get any help from the farmers who were hiding them, certain excesses were committed, something that was normal in situations like that, never the massacre that was described. Two or three days later he received a new posting on the other side of the island, to San Luis in the province of Pinar del Río. "You tell me if he had the time to commit all the atrocities he's been accused of. My husband's heart has nothing to do with his fierce face. But they had to make up demons and the bad reputation of one Merlo Sosa was passed on to my husband. I want you to believe me, I'm asking you to believe me, he's a good man." I believed her. I sincerely believed her.

One morning Pedro Morejón was handcuffed and led out of the cell. "We're taking him to Columbia military camp where the trial that was interrupted the other night will continue." I was told in the parish where I was, at the time, getting ready to go up to see them. I left immediately and met the convoy of jeeps on the way. I went into the military enclosure with them. The trial was presided over by Camilo Cienfuegos. In a tiny room into which barely fifty people could fit. The press hadn't been invited. The matter was processed in a couple of hours. The final statements lasted ten minutes at most. The deliberations behind closed doors not even that, the time it took to write a sentence, have it typewritten, and sign it. The court had found him guilty of the crimes of which he was accused and had condemned him to death. The session was closed. By midday we were on our way back to La Cabaña.

A few days later it was the turn of Luis Ricardo Grao. Before Jesús Sosa Blanco went through the same procedure, trials began to take place in La Cabaña itself and the "gallery of death" opened its doors to new guests. The space allotted to each man was reduced. The distress grew in the souls of all of them.

It was always night,
sunrise never came
to that corner of La Cabaña prison.
Light and day were a lie
appearing at the window.
They were a dirty sticky gelatin
that stuck to the skin of the soul.
It set hard and cold,
like porcelain.
Behind the gallery skylight,
the moat and open fields.
Beyond, the ocean and the sky.
Then, nothing.
The stars are grains of sand
infinitely far away
in the dense night.
The walls and floor sweat out fear
in "the gallery of death."
No one knows if it is the shadows within
 shadows

or the walls
that speak.
They aren't voices, they aren't words,
they're spoken by ghosts.
Prayers sound like drops of water
that seep into the silence
and drop into the puddle
awaiting them below.

Father, have you been there?
No, why?
It's sounds as if you have been there.
Not yet.
Words must come to you from very far away,
they must sound empty to you.
Come on, they're waiting for us.
Some get moving, others stay.
Some eyes are weeping, others burning.
We leave the prison behind us.
From the night of the gallery
to the night of the firing squad.
The last prayer, the last embrace.
How long the minutes are, how dark the hour,
how fragile the light, how humid the shadows.
One night and another night.
And the night ended up staying in my soul.

# 8

I don't remember what the date was in February, or whether it was Monday or Tuesday or Wednesday. I do remember, however, and it is still etched powerfully into my mind, the moments and scenes of inexpressible anguish that evening and that night.

There was the old routine every morning. With the first light of day, I zigzagged along Amargura Street, then San Ignacio, past the cathedral, the bandstand, to the ferryboats that came and went, went and came, crying at times and dancing at others, from Havana to Casa Blanca, from Casa Blanca to Havana. Enjoying the clear light of sunrise, the morning breeze, the sleepy voices of the early risers, when the city was beginning to awaken and stretch. Sailing in the ferryboat over the small waves of the channel, into the port and the wide-open seas of the imagination and yearnings. Going back up slowly, slowly, to the parish. At seven o'clock on the dot, going up to the altar and saying Mass for six lay sisters in nun's habits and another six in street clothes.

The midmorning routine had been changing for some weeks. Before, I stayed behind in the parish, even though I didn't have a lot to do until noon. Now, full of news to pass on up there to the prisoners, caught as they were between hope and desperation, I used to go up to La Cabaña after nine o'clock but before ten.

One time I was walking opposite the wide-open door of the military Auditory, when I heard Miguel Angel call out to me. "Father, step inside for a moment please, we have to talk." I found it strange. Our meetings were usually casual, like our conversations, informal. So "we have to talk." What did he have to tell me? There was something ugly afoot. Maybe in the best interests of good practice all the capital punishment sentences of revolutionary justice were going to be subjected automatically to revision, and maybe therefore there was a possibility of reduced sentences, several years of prison instead of the firing squad, for example. If, at midnight, the case of Pedro Morejón had been witnessed, maybe Che would preside over the court, "if only you knew what he was like . . " "Yeah, yeah, but just let it out, whatever it is you have to tell me." The sentence had been ratified and that night Pedro would be executed by firing squad.

"Uh-oh! And how has he taken it?" "He doesn't know anything yet." "What do you mean he doesn't know anything? And when were you thinking of telling him?" "We were waiting for you to arrive so that you could talk to him." "What? That I tell him? Something like 'come on Pedrito, tonight you're going to get your passport to heaven!' Are you crazy?" "Father, please, don't be like that, let's be rational." "Hey, Miguel Angel, I'll go with him wherever he has to go, but I didn't judge him, I'm not about to clean up someone else's mess. That would be the last straw." "So what do we do then?" "You're asking me? You´ll have to figure out what you're going to do."

That screwed up my day, disgusting, but you knew that at any moment the river had to flow out into the ocean, right? Holy crap, but not like that. Bite the bullet, speak softly when you wanted to scream, smile and in order to do so hide those beams at the back of your eyes, ask "how you are" instead of saying you're screwed, royally screwed, say "see you later" when the truth is that tonight it'll be goodbye forever. I reached the gallery of death. I held out my hand and asked them all, one by one, "how are you? Were you able to sleep better today? Great, fine, I'll put this in the mail this very morning." Until I got round to him and wasn't brave enough to look him squarely in the eye and hold his gaze. We must have had a group chat, I'm sure, but I don't recall about what or how keenly, I wasn't in the mood for all that. A short visit, a quick "see you later," and I left; I couldn't hold off the storm that was brewing inside me. "See you this afternoon."

I returned at about three. I went first to the Auditory, where Miguel Angel awaited. "Does he know?" "No." "When are you thinking of telling him?" "Father, why don't you go and tell him?" "It's my job to do it? No." "Whose job is it? Alfonso's or mine?" "Well, you should both go and do what you have to do once and for all, it's not right that all this time is going by and the guy doesn't know that he doesn't have a lot of it left, that's just not fair." "Father, please!" "Shit!"

In the last change of cells—"You here, you over there"—Pedro Morejón was assigned Luis Ricardo Grao as his cellmate. That way, it worked out best for both of them; they had shared this terrible experience, they knew each other's deepest secrets—the hardened and not so hardened muscles of the soul. It would have been better still if Jesús Sosa Blanco had been put in with them. I stood on the other side of the bars. Grao, afflicted with some kind of illness, getting worse by the day, spent most of the time lying on the floor.

I asked Morejón to come up to the bars. He grabbed them with both hands. I put mine on his. In a hushed voice, so that only he could hear me, I told him what had happened, that the sentence had been confirmed, why it was me who was telling him all this, because they thought it would come as not quite as much of a terrible shock, that the execution would take place that night, that if he so wished and asked me to, I would stay right by his side until the time came, that if he wanted to request anything or ask for a favor at the last minute, I'd do it in complete trust and get to working on it immediately so they complied with his wishes. He listened to me in silence, with his eyes closed, body rigid, head half-tilted. "So tonight then." Two or three words, barely any more, were all that he said. No one spoke. They had clearly realized that there was something serious in the air. The minutes became eternal. He took a deep breath and told me he wanted to be alone and didn't want anyone bothering him. I, in turn, told him I'd go down to Casa Blanca, and after my evening duties in the church I'd come back and remain until . . .

When I exited into the corridor, at that moment, a door opened out of which came a cloud of foul-smelling dust and nightclub din, including happy voices and background music. They closed it immediately when they saw me, an apparition from the hereafter, a ghost in priest's clothing. Someone, they must have thought, they or I, was in the wrong place at the wrong time. The militiamen who used to walk up and down the corridor, in charge of guarding "day and night" the gallery of death, told me what it was all about. A captain in the rebel militias, well known among the rank and file of the anti-Batista civil resistance movement, much given to night life and a troublemaker, was apprehended in a nocturnal scandal and had just been brought to La Cabaña to sleep it off and let the alcohol evaporate. He'd brought with him three women and the same number of whisky bottles.

Good heavens! It looked like that day had been made for weird things to happen, things that would have been difficult to make up, inconceivable things. And without thinking twice, better still I'd say without thinking a thousandth of a second, I opened the door and joined the party: a table, two chairs, a bed, a record player, bottles, an olive green man, ruddy-faced, an idiotic smile hanging from his face, blurry-eyed, and three scantily-clad, very curvy girls. "Hey cute little priest, help yourself to a drink, have one with us." "And what are you celebrating? The 'triumph of the revolution'?" "And you?" "I'm here because there, on the other side of the corridor"—I was very surprised he hadn't been told about it—"some men who have condemned to death are witnessing their lives being brought to an end, and one of them is going to be executed this very night." "Oh!" "Don't you think that here, at least, this isn't very appropriate, that your party seems an insult?" They weren't in control of their actions or their gestures and words. Disgraceful. Smiles enveloped their faces. "Well let's drink to their perpetual health." I didn't punch the little captain in the face because just at that moment noises were coming from outside, but I came very close to doing so. There were hideous shouts: "Father! Father! Quick! Quick!"

I ran instinctively to the first cell on the left, Morejón's. Guards and prisoners continued shouting in unison. I saw Pedro's body hanging a least a foot off of the floor, on the other side of the bars, stuck to them. I plunged my arms through the grate and grabbed him by the knees, lifted up his body as much as I could, and shouted at Grao to help me when I felt him supporting his weight. "The machete, give me the machete," I yelled at the closest guard, "that chair, bring that chair over." I stood on the chair and cut the strips of bedsheet that he had used to hang himself. The body fell to the ground, as if he were dead. "The keys, who has the keys? Quick! Bring the keys! Come on! Open that door. Does anyone know how to do artificial respiration?" Now inside the cell, I grabbed Morejón by the arms and started shaking him without thinking whether it was this or something else I should be doing. Luis Ricardo Grao, leaning over his companion, tried mouth-to-mouth resuscitation.

When he came back to life and started breathing again, it took him a few seconds to become fully conscious of what was happening, as if he were waking up from a deep sleep. "Why did they do this to me?" he complained, with his eyes and voice aimed at the gallery of death, looking like he was going to cry. "Like they insulted me, like they spat in my face." As coldly as I could I repeated the same words. "Why did you do this?"

But I didn't stop there. I opened the flood-gates and let out all the mire that had accumulated behind the dam, turning it into a reservoir. With anger, rage, a sense of failure. "What? You think you're brave, a tough guy, macho for doing this? Well, let me tell you that you're not, this is running away and running away is for cowards, not facing up to life and death head-on is for cowards. It's easy to judge when it comes to the death of others, right? There were no fears then; what different ways of showing off your strength, that of before and that just now; and did you think your friends, those in here and those in the court-yard, were going to admire you because you tied a rope around your neck? Well I can assure you that isn't the case, quite the contrary, they would have looked down on you, because the brave don't bail out and they die with their boots on, on the battlefield or before the firing squad. You have a few hours to think about it and we'll see how you behave in front of those guys who are going to execute you tonight."

Before spitting out the last of these words, I was already regretting them. By now it was too late. Silence. A compact, dense, tough silence, one of those you can feel. It was broken by Sosa Blanco from behind the bars of his cell with the strike of one of his heavyweight sayings. "Now they've heard it, boys, now they know."

I sat down on the floor next to Pedro Morejón. "Forgive me, Pedro, I shouldn't have spoken to you like that, forgive me, I know it's not easy. In your place, I'd feel the same way you do. But the thing is, life's like that, today it's someone's turn, tomorrow someone else's. We all have to go through that, we can't avoid it because we're all born, live, and die. Nobody can escape that, which is why I told you that you had to face up to it. One has to know how to die with dignity. I think the only way of achieving that is by understanding what it means to die, where death takes us, and what God's role is in all of this. Worst of all, we stuff ourselves with words but the truth is that we have no idea what is transpiring or where we are going, or who's telling the truth. We just have to walk along that path of death with our eyes shut to the moment yet open in faith, believing there's something, I have no idea what, another life, yes, that there's another life. Believing that God's waiting for us, but believing above all that God is Love that awaits us, Father, with open arms. If that is what is going to happen, what does it matter whether you die in bed or by drowning at sea or in a river or in front of a firing squad? The only thing that's important is dying with dignity and with hope, don't you think?" He didn't say much, but neither did he want me to stop talking. "Can I ask a favor, Father?" "Whatever you want." "Tonight, when they execute me, will you stay close by?" "Certainly." "Really close?" "Really close, I promise."

I went back down to the parish to preside over evening Gospel readings and prayers. Inside, deep inside beyond flesh and bone, I felt a cold dark space, blindly stumbling along, like a stone that's just been tossed out of a volcano, and I felt that something in me was inflaming the ashes of my words. I assumed it was the scoria spewed up by the day, fear of the night and of the first execution. I wasn't prepared for such predicaments and I wasn't doing a very good job. "And how is it done? Eh, God, how is it done?"

That night, the rosary in the gallery of death was quieter and slower, like an Easter procession, the mysteries of the passion and death of Christ more meticulously explained, the Ave Marias and Santa Marias more drawn out. When we finished, I passed a packet of cigarettes through the bars, as I did every night, and lit them one by one. But no one wanted to talk. Gradually they left, like owls into the night, to their own dark corners. There only remained, grasping their bars, Sosa Blanco and Morejón. I was half way between them, in the corridor. But we had forgotten all words. Or how they were used. Or what purpose they served. "Pedro, are you there?" "Yes, Chucho." Silence.

"Father, what time is it?" "Eleven twenty-five." Silence. "Pedro, are you still there?" "Yes." Silence. "Father, what time is it?" "Twelve after twelve." Silence. "It can't be much longer now, how are you Pedro?" "Fine, Chucho, fine."

At last they arrived. Captain Alfonso headed the group. He opened the door. He was going to put on the handcuffs, but I asked Alfonso to wait. "Let me hug Grao and Sosa Blanco. Goodbye, Luis. Good luck, Pedro. Goodbye, Chucho. See you soon, Pedro." They handcuffed him. We began to move. The six members of the firing squad were waiting for us at the gate of the prison. And there were three military jeeps. Several soldiers climbed into the first one, among them Major Víctor Bordón Machado. In the second, Alfonso and the driver were in the front, in the back seat, Pedro Morejón and me, and two of the firing squad sitting on the running board. The rest were in the third. The procession set off.

We made a sharp left, leaving the walled compound, crossed the bridge over the moat, and the jeeps came to a halt. I saw that a spotlight had been placed on the sidewalk running over the bridge, lighting up the moat. I saw them beginning to get out of the cars. "Here?" I thought, "the prison is right there, how can this be?" We went down a few steps to the moat. There were more than enough indications. The officials and soldiers remained standing at the bottom of the steps. It was clear;

Pedro and I had to go forward to the base of the wall. It was here. "Wait a moment," I told him, and I went over to Alfonso, at the head of the firing squad. "Are you in charge?" "Yes." "How much time do I have?" "For what?" "To speak to the guy you're going to kill." "However you see fit, it's fine."

I asked him if he was calm and told him that that was the most important thing, whether he wanted me to say something, anything, at the last moment, whether he felt at peace with God and mankind, if he wanted us to say one last prayer together. We said the Lord's Prayer. Pausing on each word. He asked me where I was going to be when they opened fire. "Right here," I replied, "one or two steps away." "Well that's it," he told me. We hugged. I was holding an eight-inch metal crucifix. "Give it a kiss, I'll be holding it like this, like I am now, with my arm outstretched. Goodbye, Pedro, we'll see each other again one day up there, beyond the stars." I stepped back two paces. I raised my arm. He looked at me.

"Squad . . . Attention! . . . Ready! . . . Aim! . . . Fire!"

The moat bellowed with the shot. The echo wailed among the walls and passageways. Pedro Morejón's body fell to the ground. I kneeled down next to him. I wetted the tip of my right-hand thumb in the oil used to anoint the sick that I had brought with me in a tube. I marked out the sign of the cross on his forehead. "By means of this holy sign of the cross, God forgives you all your sins. In the name of the Father, the Son, and the Holy Ghost. Amen, Rest in peace."

I stood up and went over to Major Víctor Bordón Machado. "Very touching, Father, very touching." "Will you just shut up? Tell me, Víctor, whose idea was it? Which fucking genius came up with the idea of bringing him here to be executed, right here, two steps away from the prison, almost right below the window of the others on death row? Can you imagine how they must be feeling? I'm going to see them now; do you want to come with me? Ah, no? I'm not surprised. Well, listen carefully to me, next time find a new location or count me out."

Alone, terribly alone, I went to the gallery of death to spend the rest of the night there, laying on the floor, with my soul half alive, half executed.

Squad . . . Fire!
Six lead pellets
go out in search of a man.
All of a sudden night fades away.
They pierce his body.
Night departs in mourning.
The six empty mouths of the rifles
mumble gray smoke,
mocking the dead man:
One less!
Indeed,
death counts from more to less,
its rosary beads.
And it veered toward less
in "the moat of the laurels"
the hope in my eyes
when it scanned new horizons.
And the hymns of hope
that burst out from my lips
when it came to the morning.

Little by little
with each "one less!"
in "the moat of the laurels"
my faith eroded.

# 9

No one knows why things happen and why they don't. The following morning, on passing the room that had become a nightclub and brothel for a few hours the previous evening, I came to ask myself what would have happened if that drunk and those whores hadn't held me up for a few minutes and, just at the moment when Pedro Morejón was trying to kill himself, I had been leaving La Cabaña. Any answer would be pure conjecture, tending toward mystery. No one knows. But one thing is true. What happened in the gallery of death that evening and that night reverberated in a new atmosphere that emerged, as if old ghosts had been shaken off and replaced by other more cheerful and friendly ones. Or by angels, although I didn't believe much in them. Or by Peace its very self, peace with a capital "P," that which was so sought after by the gaunt souls in the whirlwinds of war—that Peace of which I, during those days, was a poor beggar or petitioner as well.

It is likely that this was all influenced by the visits of Father Antonio Melo. A Cuban Franciscan getting on in years, a "man of proven virtue," a lawyer prior to becoming a monk, he came every day, morning and night, to the Calixto García Hospital, to the terminally-ill ward, with death slips hanging from the headboards of its beds. He had lengthy experience as a companion when it came to last definitive goodbyes—the apostle of good death. I had explained to him my reasons for refusing if any of those condemned men asked me to hear confession. That I wanted to keep my spirits as neutral as possible, my availability, my services, and knowing too much about them would not have helped much. And if some journalists had been a little impertinent, and bothered me with questions full of morbid curiosity, in order to safeguard the "secrecy of confession" it was best just not to know such secrets in the first place.

In order to show him where to go and, above all, introduce him to the prison staff and the condemned men, I accompanied him on his first visit. From that day on, each time that a new condemned man was brought to the gallery, I told Father Melo and, one way or another, he made plans to come up to La Cabaña. What he gave in abundance was something more than consolation, encouragement, and confession. Without any ostentation or show, he became accustomed to always providing Holy Communion, the Eucharist service. And, as I soon came to realize, no one avoided him, everyone came around to talk with him. He spoke with everybody, one by one, and they returned to their own little corners having confessed and having received communion. "Hey, Father Melo, but those types of people who know nothing at all about religion are coming. They don't know how to pray, they've never been 'practicing,' they're just baptized and that's it, as they themselves acknowledge." "My son, God doesn't ask about such things. Christ came in search of lost sheep, which we all are, and you've no idea how happy each time is when He meets one of them. Don't bother with such mean-spirited comments and ask them tonight, after the rosary, how many want to take communion tomorrow morning." I did so and the response was overwhelming—all of them.

With a detector of positive and negative vibrations we could perhaps have been able to see how, each time Father Melo left the gallery of death, it was full of life. It was a natural kind of life distinct from that of the body's birth-life-death. Personally, I felt obliged to recognize that he dispelled a lot of shadows from my mind and conveyed to me great tranquility and star-filled skies.

The Auditory did not disappoint the high-ranking leaders. It began to work seriously on the trials. Cases were heard in the galleries of death every night. Some of them lasted more than one evening. "What's his name has told me, I've found out, that he's being taken to trial tonight and he's asking for me to be present. But I don't understand to what purpose. I have no say in these trials, I'm not a judge or prosecutor or lawyer or witness; I sit down and nobody asks me my opinion or makes me speak. But he wants me there. OK, tell him I'll be there." In such a fashion, I altered the rule book. I added a quick visit to the trials after the rosary. The trials often went on until one or two in the morning. I attended if there was a feel in the air, in the gestures and the attitudes of the participants that they were dealing with death sentences.

You don't have to be an expert in the law and legal procedures in order to appreciate fairly obvious and serious irregularities in some judicial processes. The trials of the victorious rebel army—not the people's trials, as was said on more than one occasion—presented there, in La Cabaña, numerous hearings plagued with defects. Starting with the fact that none of the three men who served as judges presiding over them were really judges or even shark lawyers. One could see that from a mile away. The prosecutors, however, and especially De la Fuente, were good at their assignment—insofar as their task consisted of accusing, hammering home the accusation with evidence, although sometimes the proof was reduced to little more than shouts and a blunt banging of their fists on tables and calling for the corresponding sentences, the harsher the better. A zeal for doing their work well? A hot-headed aversion toward the accused? Ambition, a desire to get ahead? I could never discern in any of them either serenity or balance or equidistance when it came to expressing their judgment or opinion; nor an ounce of human understanding or kindness. I approached Duque Estrada more than once. "Hey, Miguel Angel, if not in the name of justice itself, nor even in the good name of the revolution, you should do something to conceal those anomalies. They're too obvious, man, you're running the risk of the foreign press circling like vultures to disparage your brand-new justice, and then the fame of the revolution." I don't know whether they were simply indifferent to what I was telling them, or if the ruses to dress up appearances were in effect ruses and nothing else.

Ah, the defense lawyers. Yes, they deserve a separate paragraph. I can't tar them all with the same brush. There were decent and earnest ones, fewer in number. But there were others . . . It was painful to see them in action. Birds of prey, so much so that it seemed engraved into their souls. It was enough to feel shame, embarrassment, rage, and anger. The relatives of a defendant were always willing to pay for a defense lawyer, in the hope he would be good and effective. In order to hire him, they were willing to go hungry, sell their home, go into debt, anything. The lawyers knew full well their limitations—like having to walk on a surface of molten hot lava—and they knew that in most, if not all, the cases the sentences were fixed and decided before the trial even began. They understood that they were going to lose, that in all likelihood this was their only alternative. Lose the trial and charge a big fee. One warned the relatives, but it was useless. Over and over again they slipped and fell into the broken nets of shattered hopes.

'Theater' offers its authors a wide range in which to proceed: tragedy, drama, comedy, farce, opera, zarzuela. The range of the revolutionary trials was more restricted: tragedy and drama. However, the case put together against Otto Meruelo was, before even treading the boards on the stage itself and at the closing curtain, a farce, but without even rising to the level of comedy. It was a show trial with the aim of making one man suffer unnecessarily and the rest laugh. "But, why do they need to do that Miguel Angel? Serious matters should be treated seriously. Or are there any special reasons—I'd appreciate you telling me if there are—to hold a trial in the La Cabaña theater, with a specially invited audience, and, I wouldn't be surprised, some gruesome special effects by the prosecutor?" "The thing is, Father, have they forgotten the stomach cramps and intestinal pain that we suffered thanks to this man's plans for our lunch? He should pay!" Otto Meruelo, in front of the microphone a bold and earnest defender of the truth according to Batista, a paladin of the blatant lie and the low blow, paid with the same currency, wetting himself night after night. Without any need whatsoever and merely out of a desire to see him suffer, his trial dragged on. I didn't miss any session at the request of the protagonist of the tragic charade—the defendant. He was, by the way, the most broken of all those to sit on the bench when the prosecutor asked for the death penalty—in the full knowledge that the sentence agreed on beforehand was a prison term.

The trials increased the numbers in the gallery of death and the firing squad reduced them. The absurd notification of the execution transpiring as far removed from "the priest" as possible was never repeated. An official, from the Auditory or the prison itself, was in charge of informing either the condemned men or me. Not always, unfortunately, with sufficient time for me to prepare a proper farewell, delivered either in person or written, or to collect a bundle of clothes and some small possessions they wanted their families to have. Should there be a "case review" hearing, Che always presided. Sometimes it went beyond just ratification of the previously dictated sentence, and included the order that "the execution will take place this very night." It caused additional and, I think, unnecessary suffering. "Why isn't this applied in all cases? Why, Commander?"

I asked Che after one of these hearings, but I didn't get any response.

The second, as well as all the other executions from February to June 1959, took place in the moat of the laurels. I've been told by several friends, among them Father Miguel Angel Loredo and Salvador Subirá, a seminarian, who spent part of their prison sentence in La Cabaña, that during their time there the executions took place in the moat at the foot of the prison. It is possible. I understand that the mistreatment of prisoners never diminished; on the contrary, it increased in intensity and cruelty. We used to leave the actual "castle" for the open space outside, and then double back toward the monument of Christ, and down to Casa Blanca. Next to the checkpoint, before entering again the walled enclosure, to a small square, the widest space within the walls. At the foot of a big one, over thirty feet in height and ten feet away, there was a well-implanted pole, firmly anchored in the earth for a long time, the legacy of past cruelties. It was where Pedro Morejón could have been taken. Near there, several feet away, I attended to fifty-four other men in the last moments of their lives. They could have done without the pole. "They're going to tie you to it, or do you prefer to die without being trussed?" "No, no, I don't want to be tied up." Similarly: "They're going to cover your eyes, or do you prefer to die without your being blindfolded?" The two questions became routine. And the answer was always the same. Stand up straight, head held high, eyes open. There was really nothing more they could do.

Duque Estrada was waiting for me one morning. "Father, I have to tell you something." "Tell me." "I've just found out that Commander Guevara gave an order last night related to the executions." "Come on, tell me what it's about." "He ordered that no one, no one at all, was to be executed without you being present." "I've always been present." "By all accounts, he wants to make sure it will continue to be so in the future. And do you know why? Well, it's said that you hypnotize them before facing the firing squad and that's why things run so smoothly." "Screw that! Che doesn't believe in such stupid ideas." "And why not?" "We already know that he doesn't believe in the mysteries of religion, 'opium', as those Marxists call it." "But hypnosis is part of science, right? Why wouldn't he believe in that?" "Because it's not true, damn it, it's not true."

And of course it wasn't true. And it was equally the case that Che didn't consider me to be a hypnotist. He would have asked me. What happened was that everything was going well, effortlessly, without any scandal, without any problem, and that was good for them. Anything on the contrary could leak out to the press and create problems. Possibly Che, with the already inflated ego of a successful guerrilla, would have preferred to know that "his" executed men, while dying, were screaming and kicking up a fuss, and cursing his name and that of Fidel and those of all the Sierra bearded ones. But would that have been a good thing for a revolution that was being consolidated, putting down its roots? It was better that they died without making a sound, like docile little lambs.

It's true that no one explained what was going on with those firing squads—perhaps least of all me. Prison teaches you a lot. Naturally, there are lessons about the lack of freedom and the loss of any hope of ever regaining it within a predictable time frame. That changes your perspective on life and your outlook. It's possible that one's first reactions on being imprisoned are surprise and anger. But insofar as one realizes anger doesn't get you anywhere, that vital inner energy we possess seeks out instinctively other ways of expressing itself and getting on with things. He who manages to make the best of what little time remains will develop survival tactics and attempt to become a positive force within the still the constraining prison environment. He who lets himself be overcome by despair begins to develop an encompassing dark moss around his soul, and that can be very bad for him. They all possess one thing in common: they want to live and in order to do so they refuse to think about death. As if the less they think about it, the more they can hold it at bay.

To anyone condemned to die within a few days' stretch, whether as a result of a terminal illness or the sentence of a trial, the lights are switched off on the stage or stages on which that person lived; their past collapses. And what happens then if no one knows what's beyond the gate of death? If no one tells them that there is indeed something there and what it is like? It's true that "hope is the last thing ever lost," that even if you lose your faith and love, there's still hope. But hope, like all other emotions, is a pro-active virtue; one must know what to hope for in order to cultivate it. That's where I came in. And I didn't know what to tell them because I didn't believe in either heaven or hell—despite what I'd been taught. And I told them that the afterlife is a mystery, an infinite mystery for me as well. That God was also a mystery, a mystery that was light, that was truth, that was energy, that was love, that was life, above all, or as a sum of everything. That was Life—both mystery-Life here and mystery-Life beyond this world. And, apart from that, I spoke to them about Christ, about blessedness. I shared with them a few parables, "the king of the heavens is like . . . ." I told them about a few "miracles" in which mystery was also interwoven, questions without replies as to "how that could be?" and I spoke to them about the example of Christ's life and a lot about His death. I spoke to them about that, provided them with company, and suffered with them. And when they cried, which did happen now and again for one reason or another, I cried. And when they laughed on remembering something or while telling a joke, I laughed. But I didn't hypnotize them; I don't know how to hypnotize. I was upset they said that because I believed, despite all my incredulities, that someone or something that wasn't me was present. And I thought calling it hypnotism was akin to fetching the water of explanation from a false ditch.

I don't remember his name. He was a police sergeant, stocky, not given to talking much. He was placed before the firing squad alongside four co-accused colleagues on account of the events at 7 Humboldt Street in which, it was alleged, Carbó Serviá had been eliminated. As I took him to be the strongest and calmest of the five, I told him his colleagues would be executed before him. Thus it was that I arranged them, as I did almost always when there was more than one execution. I determined the order according to how I viewed their spirits. It was the order in which I would accompany them one by one to their rendezvous with the infinite "zero" point and time. From the place in which they were waiting, the others could not see anything, but they could hear the voices issuing the order to fire and the shots. It was awful. But it was unavoidable.

Captain Alfonso was in charge of the firing squad that night. Like all those who preceded him,

I spent what I considered to be the necessary time with the victim beforehand. We possibly smoked a cigarette together, I don't recall. We chatted, we prayed slowly the age-old "Our Father," then the last embrace, a kiss of the image of Christ on the cross, and the "until we meet again up there." I stepped back. Alfonso gave the order. The body fell to the ground. We approached it. He wasn't dead. He was moaning "Father, Father." Visibly disoriented, Alfonso wasn't able to put him out of his misery. I was shaking and, with gestures, urged Alfonso to shoot him in the head. Without even turning toward the dying man, and who knows if his eyes were closed or covered owing to his condition, Alfonso fired and God knows where the bullet went. The dying man was still moaning, "Father, Father." People gathered around the firing squad, including Duque Estrada and some other officials. I went up to Duque Estrada: "He's been shot already, the sentence has been fulfilled, take him to hospital." "Father, Father," continued the moans. "No, he was sentenced to death and he has to die here." Alfonso fired a second shot. Another bullet wasted. "Father, Father." I grabbed Alfonso by the wrist, moved his hand over to the man's head. "Pull it, pull it now." He pulled the trigger. The body shook on the ground. Breathing intermittently, trembling, I administered the last rites. Rest in peace. I left without looking at, or saying goodbye, to anyone.

On the way back to my monastery, near the Asturian Center, heading for Teniente Rey Street, I almost had an accident with another car.

Sometimes, Father Estanislao Sudupe used to fall asleep with a book or magazine in his hand and the light switched on. I saw the light in his room and went in without knocking, thinking he was awake. "I want to say confession, tonight I killed a man." "What did you say?" "That I killed a man." "Explain yourself." It took me a long time to calm down. I only barely managed to do so. I didn't go to bed. I went up to the roof of the monastery to contemplate the stars and cry with them.

Shut up! We're praying!
Like a flash of lightning,
like a bolt of thunder.
The gallery shakes.
A shout bounces off the stones
and disappears into the night.
Silence.
We carry on praying.
Steps in water with bare feet,
voices muffled by rags,
flashlights switched off,
the rosary goes on,
walking and walking around the same square,
"God save you Mary, holy Mary . . .
God save you Mary, holy Mary."
Some just move their lips,
they don't know the words.,
and yet they're praying.
Words are the least of it,
I tell them,

they need not move their lips,
and they can close their eyes.
You pray with heart
and with your feet and with your hands.
When you truly pray,
it's your soul and your body your entire life
that pray,
what someone once was
and is today.
Praying cleanses the soul
like clean water the body.

What are we praying for? someone asks.
Each person knows what they are praying for.
I'm praying to ask for a miracle.
For cotton to turn into lead?
Won't you be praying in vain?
So, what do I ask for?
That at that time He is beside you.
Praying, I tell them,
Helps to clear a way forward
and open up doors.
We carry on praying.
When we finish the rosary
a deep breath is heard,
as if we had arrived exhaustedly at a finish line
and were sitting down to rest.
Relaxing.
For those that smoke, I light
their cigarette.

# 10

And now? It's a sign that's something's wrong when, at two or three in the morning, you ask yourself "what do I do now?" It sounds like crazy talk. Because two in the morning for someone who is not going off to work, to begin a new working day, is supposedly the path to bed with head and eyes nodding from the heavy burden of a day's weariness. However, I was seeking out other alternatives, stress-free sleep alternatives. I invented anesthetics to help me fall into a deep sleep as soon as my body hit the sack. I was afraid of going to bed, of sleep, of the "dreams" that began to inhabit my sleep. One night I accompanied my parents, father and mother, condemned to death for I don't know what, to the firing squad. Another night, the person led to the wall was Pope Pius XII. I wasn't really all that interested in what Sigmund Freud would have said about these dreams. It was horrible waking up with a scream, my body shaking as if zapped by an electric shock.

One of my anesthetic ploys was pressing the accelerator pedal to the floor, until the car reached its maximum speed, recklessly, on the point of uncontrollably skidding and having a deadly accident on the new expressway to Cojimar and the beaches of Tarará and Santa María del Mar. I wanted to see if such tension would suppress what I just described. Another was drinking whisky straight from the bottle. That man who prepared rabbit fricassee for his friend in prison had given me a crate of "White Horse" Scotch, twelve bottles to be shipped one-by-one to his friend. "But, what on earth are you thinking? That I'm going to start a bar in La Cabaña prison? Come on now! Take this back to wherever you got it." "You keep it and do whatever you see fit with it." I didn't know that damned grief was an expert swimmer in the swimming pools of whisky. I imbibed it on more than one occasion, without reaching Herculean proportions, and was able to sleep the few hours after midnight. The result was that I began to like what previously used to annoy me because it tasted like medicine. This became true to the point, possibly, that I was showing signs of being an alcoholic. But as a cure for grief, I found nothing, absolutely nothing.

Sometimes I searched out an empty old rickety bed in the quarters of the troops consigned to the prison, and tried to catch a couple of hours of sleep. At least if some of the young guys didn't grab me for a quick chat. They were, in general, reserved, little prone to talking outside their own group. They had all heard me once or twice when I went to see the condemned men for prayers or to answer their questions, or simply telling them about or commenting on news of the outside world. They respected and awaited me like an oracle. Some, by nature more open and outgoing, told me stories about the guerrilla warfare in the mountains, and, with special delight, their adventures in Havana, dragged there in the tidal wave of victory. There was one—and his first name was Adán (Adam)!—who went on and on about his amorous exploits or, more accurately, his cheap hook-ups. "Father, I think I'm sick," he confessed one night. "I'm not a doctor, but if you want to tell me about it, let it out." "Tonight I was impotent." "What happened?" "Well, I was with a woman and I couldn't do anything." "With the first or with the last one?" "With the last one?" "And with how many had you slept beforehand?" "Seven." "What you've done is being a reprobate!" They all liked going to prostitutes, but none more so than Adán. It never occurred to me to warn them that this was a sin. Was Adán capable of sinning? They weren't all like him, that's for sure.

Or I went over to the wall and sat down to gaze at the city lights and the darkness of the ocean. Waiting for the night to fade and for the light to replace the shadows little by little. What could I do to make that light permeate me and supplant those other shadows in my soul?

Some afternoons, and on the suggestion of Monsignor Evelio Díaz, the acting archbishop of Havana, no less, I went to a movie theater to see the first session on its listings. I almost never saw a film all the way through, because I used to fall asleep, gently swaying in the hammock of its music and colors. Yet on waking up and scurrying outside, hurrying back to La Cabaña, I noticed I was more rested than if I had had a sleep in bed.

"Some come and others go." "In the rush of life" for the poet José Selgas; in the parade of death for me. The doors of the four cells in the gallery used to open and close, some men left and never returned, others came to fill the vacancy that the departed left behind, to await desperately, to look back toward the past and bid it farewell, to look toward the future and scrutinize its mysteries. The atmosphere continued to be that of "don't waste time in yearning and rebelling over what is gone; there in no going back so seek another way out—which there is." The resignation of the defeated animal? The acceptance by the intelligent rational being?

They all passed this along to each other. They used to speak with Father Melo and, with one single exception, asked to take part in the communicants' group the following day. Every afternoon the rosary gave me the opportunity to comment on, and apply, the Gospel to the life experienced by them before on the outside and to what was being undergone now behind bars. Jesus was friend and brother; He who had lived and died teaching how to live and die. Applications to real life when it was coming to an end: a slide and fall into emptiness or a trampoline and acrobatic jump into Life. I was disseminating a faith I did not have. And I used to smile so that they would not realize I was crying.

The firing squad experienced a change that brought some relief to the officials assigned to organizing the executions, although not to the prisoners who were to be executed or to the rest of the actors in the macabre event. Captain Alfonso Zayas was able to act like a hero in the mountains or in the city of Santa Clara, but once in charge of a squad obliged to kill in cold blood, his froze in its veins. He did it because it was his duty, but one could see, despite all of his attempts to hide it, his repugnance. Nor did the man who substituted for him on some nights really meet the necessary thuggish qualifications. Che Guevara, of whom his enemies have said so often that his hands were stained with the blood of those executed in La Cabaña, never even appeared to give the order "Fire!" or to put anyone out of his misery. But one day, one night, a sinister man appeared, a born killer, one of those who takes pleasure in it. I imagine that for him it was close to an orgasm. At the head of the firing squad, he was a true prophet of death. A nasty piece of work, a fugitive from justice in his native United States, he had enlisted in the Cuban revolution because, in his mind, being a revolutionary and being a butcher of human beings were synonymous. His name was Herman Marks. There is no choosing one's traveling companions at certain moments of one's life. Individuals like Marks spread their filth and taint anyone who comes into contact with them. One feels ashamed to have even been near them. I'll never forget his face and his gestures that afternoon. He approached and hugged me because that night there would be a feast of seven—seven!—executions.

At least that night I was able to enjoy the close company of a friend, Father Tomás Olazábal. He'd offered to help out as my acolyte whenever I may have felt overwhelmed. I called him that night. He led the rosary and stayed with me in the long interminable darkness, in which the clock seemed like it was refusing to move and tell accurate time. He didn't, nor could he, serve as any consolation, but I felt and appreciated his presence as a friend. It was as when I passed another night with my friend Father Mariano Errasti as well. Similarly, there was the one with Monsignor Eduardo Boza Masvidal, parish priest of Caridad and later auxiliary bishop of Havana, expelled from Cuba by Fidel and an illustrious exile among the illustrious exiles. He had asked me if it would be possible to attend the execution of someone from a family he knew.

Luis Ricardo Grao was one of the seven names on that list. Of the three from the Palacio de los Deportes on January 28, he'd been preceded by Pedro Morejón and he was second, with Jesús Sosa Blanco having to wait only a few more nights. How Grao managed to arrive alive that night no one knows. He had for some days been slowing fading away, like the flickering flame of a candle, at death's door, but not quite extinguished. He was not eating a lot, he was not speaking much, and he was smiling from somewhere way beyond his shutter-slatted eyes. He received communion every day and that afternoon, as soon as he saw me arrive at the gallery, he called out to ask if I would give communion in the evening as well, even though that would be twice in one day. He thought that it would provide him strength when it came to leaving for the firing squad. I would have gladly turned up with the cup full of hosts, all for him.

I behaved cruelly to some extent with him during his final moments. He was clearly finished, very ill, a poor physical specimen, and yet at the same time the calmest of the seven, a giant in spirit. On the one hand, I felt the obligation to spare him any more suffering, to put him out of his agony, leading him to the firing squad first. And yet I reserved the last spot for him. I let him know so and asked him to impart some of his fortitude to his companions as they were waiting for me to collect them one by one to be led like sheep to the slaughterhouse. He agreed. I'm sure he did so perfectly, maybe with words, maybe in silence, it doesn't matter.

When he was all alone, we didn't need any more time or extra support for his spirits and his feet to remain firm. It was for me one of the most emotional goodbyes and embraces. His gaze was fixed on the cross that Father Tomás was holding high in his right hand. The orders were being shouted out emphatically. The path to death was opening up. "Fire!" Six bullets reached the spot where Luis Ricardo Grao was. He awaited them standing strong. And he was still upright when silence followed the deafening noise. Shot through with bullets and still standing? Was it possible? We approached him. Was he alive? Was he dead? He was standing. So steadfast that not even the impact of the six bullets could topple him? Or untouched by the lead because the young guys in the firing squad, knowing who they were executing, preferred not to aim to kill? From the front and looking at his clothes there was no sign of any impact. At the back, though, one could see the holes from where the bullets had exited and blood was gushing out. But I didn't look and so I didn't know. The official aimed his pistol at the temple and put him out of his misery. He fell down in a heap. I got down on my knees to administer the last rites. Rest in peace, friend. And muttering, how I envy you, young man.

A few nights later, I told Jesús Sosa Blanco that his turn had come. He was expecting it, we were already surprised, both of us, that so many had gone before him. He'd said goodbye to his Amelia and daughters. I didn't want to be present at their last kiss. He didn't leave any loose ends behind. He asked to be allowed to be presentable—washed, clean-shaven, clean underwear—in order to meet his death. He stepped to one side to talk to Marcial, the "rebel" with whom he had developed a sense of trust and who was a renowned marksman. Off to the side, but speaking loudly enough for us all to hear, he asked Marcial to make sure he was part of the firing squad that night. He wanted him to fire the critical bullet; he demanded no less that Marcial would swear to fire to the right, to the far right, at his heart. "Here, take a good look, see? This is where my heart is." Then he called out to me. He also wanted me to do him a favor. "Do you see these shoes?"—at this point he was addressing me in the familiar *tu*—"look at them, they're new, never been worn, I got them for New Year's Eve, but didn't wear them. I don't know why not, better, that way I'll wear them on the eve of my death. But I don't want to be buried with them. I prefer to go six feet under without any shoes, so take them off when I'm dead and tomorrow, in La Cabaña or in Havana, give them away to a beggar. Make sure that he has big feet, otherwise they'll be of no use, but don't tell him who they belonged to.

I mean, he may not want to put them on." "Now it's my turn to ask, and why are you doing this?" "I got the idea of playing a small joke on Fidel and his revolution, they'll execute me, but they haven't beaten me." Once the rosary was over, he wanted to say a few words to his companions in misfortune. Not much, just a "see you later." It was no pep talk. Nor did he remind them of the old times. He spoke about looking toward the future. "It's the only thing of any interest," he repeated several times. "I'm going first. I'll wait for you there."

The time had come, we had said the "Our Father"—"The last one. Do you remember the first time you asked me to say it with you? You have no idea how much I appreciate that"—and I was going to hug him and say goodbye when he grabbed my hand. "Another favor, I want you to do me another favor, my last request. I want to say a couple of words to the soldiers who are going to execute me." I was of two minds. "What's this guy thinking about now?" It was not in my power to decide, but nor did the brute at the head of the firing squad have any right to do so. "On one condition," I told him, "that you speak in a polite way and you make it brief, I'm going to be here and if you don't comply, I'll cut you off." He didn't say much and he did so in a very moving way. He told them that the Cuba he loved and that they loved was one and the same, and that he had not known how to make it happy. They should please treat it well and make it happy.

He shouted "Long live Cuba!" and fell silent. He was ready to receive "sister death."

I placed the sacramental oil on his forehead. Then I took off his shoes, a huge pair, made of crisp, shiny leather. "And what's all that about?" someone asked me. "He gave them to me," I answered. No one said a word. And I stepped back with the shoes in my hands.

I didn't have to walk very far the following day to find a beggar with big enough feet who was overjoyed to receive Jesús Sosa Blanco's shoes, convinced I had bought them to give to him. Paradoxes of life. Sosa Blanco's "mischievous spirit," concealed in the shoes that he wore for the first time to look elegant just before his death, mysteriously continued to roam cheerfully the old streets of Old Havana. I don't know for how long. The Sosa Blanco that I knew in La Cabaña—the chess player, the talker, he of the coconut heart, white and sweet on the inside.

He asked for a glass of water
when they came to get him
to take him to the firing squad.
Sip by sip, in silence, he drank it.
The water that flowed those nights
in the drinking fountains of La Cabaña
was bitter.
Neither tart nor salty,
bitter.
Bitter from bitterness.
A bitterness that appeared at twilight
in the crevices of the soul.
A bunch of broken voices,
of lights that did not know what light was for,
of intentions baked in frigid minds,
of lost steps in the quagmire,
of memories and oversights that scratch and
        hurt,
of a thick gray sadness,
of the revulsion that precedes vomiting,

of fatigue with a wayward rhythm,
of windows that one wished
one had never opened,
of a sharp pain on one side,
of the desire to crawl up and die in a corner,
of a revolting sensation of failure,
of weariness,
of feeling like shouting at God
"is this what you made us for?"
the bitterness of La Cabaña
on the way to the firing squad.

# 11

Easter that year was March 30 to April 5. The Monday of that week I met Fidel Castro in person. Che Guevara did not set up the meeting, but he did have something to do with it. At that time, during one casual meeting, the commandant told me he would like to have a chat. "When? Where?" "Could you come along to command headquarters tomorrow morning sometime?" "That's fine. See you tomorrow."

Surprises that surprise one even more on account of not having been announced and because in themselves they were very difficult to imagine. Che wanted me to serve as a kind of bridge between him and three priests. I had spoken to him of them and he wanted a meeting. They were three quite interesting intellectuals: Father Hilario Chaurrondo, a member of the Congregation of the Mission (Paules or Vincentians), a famed preacher and organizer of missionary campaigns the length and breadth of Cuba, born in Navarre,

Spain. Father Angel Gaztelu, a diocesan priest, the author of several published works of poetry, was the parish priest of Espíritu Santo, Cuba. And Father Ignacio Biain, a Franciscan, a teacher at the "Universidad del Aire"—a popular educational radio show in Cuba in the 1940s and 1950s—and editor in chief of the journal *La Quincena*, was born in Gipuzkoa, the Basque Country, Spain. All three lived in Old Havana, carried Basque last names, and hobbled along to the left. In other words, their thought was of a leftist persuasion. In order to motivate myself to setting up the meeting with them, I explained that I should also be present. I wanted to speak with them and hear their thoughts and opinions on the revolution, its spirit, its laws, and the reforms that had been announced, the justice that was being applied, and so on.

I only spoke to Father Biain, whom I saw every day at lunchtime because we were members of the same religious community. And I didn't even tell him that it was anything formal and serious; rather, should their paths ever cross, Fidel would be delighted to meet him because he had heard great things about him. I didn't even say that to the other two. The thing is, it seemed to me and knowing Che, that behind such silky words there lurked more shadowy intentions. He was not interested in any moral support, or in any opinions, whether similar to his or not. What he sought to do with them was to create one or two or three cysts or tumors within the tissue and underneath the skin of the Church. Already by that time I was not exactly enamored by this institution that was so hierarchical, closed, and anchored to immovable prejudices and doctrine. Running the Church was the purview of a few individuals giving orders and the rest following them and keeping quiet, and I doubted that Christ would like this church. Yet my indifference still was not so great as to leave half-open the door so that a wolf could sneak in to organize treacherous cubbyholes within.

When I went to the meeting with the commandant in his command headquarters, my nocturnal rambles from the prison to the firing squad wall had already hardened my feet, if not my soul, which continued to bleed. I needed a break, and it occurred to me that Easter offered an unmissable opportunity to silence the guns, to rest, and to meditate for a few days. I thought about telling Che. But a voice came into my head while we were chatting: "Che is going to refuse you permission, he doesn't believe in such things, don't even speak to him about that, why don't you go to Fidel directly?"

By Palm Sunday I still hadn't managed to establish any direct contact and set up a meeting. So I said to myself: "Tomorrow I'll find out where he is and if he's in Havana, I'll just show up like I did on the Epiphany at Che's residence, and let's just see if I have the same luck."

I asked my contacts in La Cabaña and found out that Fidel had spent the night and could be found during the morning at such and such a house, in such and such a street, in the Vedado neighborhood. I would find him there, as I would Celia Sánchez, if I was also interested in her. No, I wasn't interested in Celia, it was Fidel with whom I wanted to speak. "If he agrees to see you or not, that's another matter, but go along and good luck." I parked the car in an adjacent street and walked over to the house. How strange. No police cars in the immediate vicinity or armed guards at the entrance; no protection that I could see. I knocked on the door. A militiaman opened it. There were two of them and they were both carrying machine guns. "Good morning, I don't have an appointment, I didn't ask for a meeting, I hope for one and that's why I'm here, would you be so kind as to let Commandant Fidel Castro know that the parish priest of Casa Blanca would like to speak with him?"

And so it happened that he could see me. "Come along," and they led me to a room converted into an office, a large table and several chairs, at which Fidel Castro was working and from which he received me; and from which a half hour later I would be dismissed—and not in a very good way, let's say. But I must be honest and note that before seeing his face and holding out my hand in greeting, I was admiring him like I had never done before, whether through reading articles or listening to the stories of the Sierra, or watching open-mouthed his appearances in front of the cameras and paying close attention until nodding off during his notoriously lengthy discourses. I admired him now because there was no other head of state on earth without a castle or palace or tower replete with offices, ostentation and surrounded by luxuries and protection. In contrast, Fidel ate, worked, and slept in a modest house, befitting of a middle-class family, without much space for company or a security entourage. It is what you see, I thought. If this is an example of what's coming, we can congratulate ourselves. You're doing better than all right, Fidel. You're doing better than okay, Cuba. Unfortunately, that was no such example; I had just slipped on a banana peel and fallen down with a thump for the umpteenth time. It was, plainly and simply, a prudent hideout designed to mislead because the enemy never slept. The dreams and promises had started to fade soon for some, as early as the spring of 59, and someone could be lying in wait.

Once we had both sat down, without any time to explain the reasons and the purpose that had led me to him, he surprised me with another of his very particular facets. By all accounts, in Fidel's head there was no room for the idea that, "if someone comes to see me it's because they want to tell me something," because it was instead the opposite that, "whoever comes to see me, comes to listen to me." I'm not sure what he was occupied with at the time, probably something related to agrarian reform. He traversed Cuba's farmlands, not to sing a *guajira* or a *son montuno*—had he ever sung? Nor was it to recite any verses oozing with sweet, honey-colored beauty. Instead it was to draw up castles of numbers, numbers that illustrated the terrible distribution of lands and the wealth carved out of them by the Americans, numbers concerning the future wealth that, to the benefit of the people, they were now going to create through our inspiration and guidance, that of the revolution. He traveled from east to west on the island, jumping fences and barriers, over the flatlands and the mountains, through sugar-cane fields, cattle farms, and coffee plantation—numbers, numbers, and more numbers. "So, what brings you here?"

I had prepared a few things beforehand that his numbers had erased from my mind. By fits and starts, stunned by so many numbers, I said: "You know, Commander, in La Cabaña . . . the revolutionary trials . . . the firing squad . . . I believe, Commander, during Easter season the firing squad should cease, we should make do with the great death—He who died for all of us on the cross. I've come to ask you to suspend the executions during these days, for the love of Christ, Commander."

Holy cow! What a reaction. I was struck by a

bolt of lightning, Fidel being perfectly capable of ordering me to be shot that very night. How he shouted. "What makes you think, who gave you permission to get involved in things that don't concern you, what gives you the right?" I got up, "Goodbye, goodbye," went to the door and disappeared, running to the car.

The following morning, Fidel's shouting was ricocheting off of the cobblestones of La Cabaña as I was making my way to the prison. Duque Estrada was calling out to me. "What happened yesterday, Father?" "Nothing, why do you ask?" Because Fidel Castro had sent him greetings and let him know that there would be no executions this week. "What?" "We're taking a break until next week, no trials, no firing squad." I told him what had happened. "And you're surprised he reacted like that?"

I dreamed of a squadron of angels,
carrying rifles,
executing children.
I dreamed about my father and mother being
executed.
I dreamed about Pope Pius XII being executed.
I dreamed about friends being executed.
I dreamed about the green body
of a giant that had been executed
hanging over the blue of the Caribbean sea.
I dreamed that I had been executed.
I dreamed about a firing squad
on the stone sidewalk
of a street in Jerusalem
on the way to a nearby mountain.
At three o'clock in the afternoon I dreamed
about
a discharge of gunfire,
I ran up the mountain,
I dreamed about three empty crosses.

I never dreamed about
a bridge
and a green promenade on the other side.
I did not dream about smiling stars.
I did not dream about the northern lights.
I did not dream about a tree full of lights
when evening came around.
I did not dream about two young people
          holding hands,
walking,
singing,
dreaming . . .

# 12

The following week the Resurrected Christ was once again bearing his cross in the Stations of the Cross of La Cabaña. At the time, the case of Ariel Lima was being heard. Like all of them, this one had a profound impact on me, and yet it was special because of its unusual elements. To the best of my knowledge, in stating this, I don't think Ariel lied to me, and I acted in his defense in good faith, albeit mistakenly. I realized that when composing the first draft of this text. I'm not bothered about having been taken in. I've always been easy prey for other people's pain, my compassion quickly stirred. I'd rather be thought of as stupid than mean.

Nor was the age of the young guy the most striking thing. He was the youngest man of the fifty-five men I attended to during the executions. By a long way. The average age of those executed in La Cabaña during that time was forty, more or less. Two or three were around thirty. Ariel had turned twenty-one just before he was led away and killed by a firing squad. Now with the passing of time, I cannot remember whether he had the face of a child naturally or if it was fear that made his appearance and speech childlike. It made me believe he was under eighteen, and that prompted me to take the steps that I did on his behalf.

The name Ariel Lima also brings to mind other memories that, on resurfacing, cloud everything, like mud deposited at the bottom of a pond. I refer to memories related to torture as a tool and a practice for gathering information, breaking wills, and maintaining order and security. Or when it is merely to punish and carry our reprisals, how appalling! It has always existed and history is full of torturers and the tortured, no exercise of power or government can be sure to have totally clean hands. Those who argue to the contrary are lying. Even the hands and the elbows and the arms of the Church are dripping with innocent blood spilled on torture racks set up by its "Holy Inquisition!"

The workshops that turned out revolutionaries knew just how many immature, charming, malleable young dreamers there were—young men who arrived at their doors aiming to be heroes, who would throw in the towel and even betray the cause at the first hint of torture. They accept them despite all this, nourish their silly dreams of grandeur and then launch them on the path to adventure and abandon them to their fate if they fall into the clutches of the beast. These are snot-nosed adolescents emulating Robin Hood or Zorro, ready to repeat or surpass their exploits. Ariel Lima was one of these young dreamers, just another one, nothing out of the ordinary. He was, perhaps, a little braver than other companions, he resisted more, and he even played with the fire of heroism. But it ended up burning him. Nobody asked him to be a hero; he sought that out himself. He was sentenced and taken to the firing squad before the rose bush could bloom in his heart. He gave in to torture and to weakness.

It is a sign of adolescence to confuse civil resistance with revolutionary struggle or subversive action, to confound being an urban guerrilla with a bit of an adventure. Playing with fire and not getting burned, outsmarting the net of laws and bylaws that regulate public life, raising a ruckus, fleeing, and forcing the police to give chase. In other words, playing, while thinking at the same time you're contributing something to a noble cause. They let themselves be taken in at school or in their neighborhood, seduced by the clandestine and furtive atmosphere into which they were introduced. Today they would distribute some pamphlets, tomorrow they would daub some walls with libertarian graffiti, another day they would throw stones at some storefront windows—and they got used to all that. They were given literature prepared ad hoc to read. "Read it, you can help save the homeland, get ready, we young people will build a new world, for a free Cuba," and so on.

That's how Ariel Lima got his start. He never told me how much he was involved in clandestine matters or how high up he was in the organization, nor in what specific assignments or activities he had been involved. He let it be implied that he was "someone," a man of trust. Until one day the police caught him, gave him a good beating from head to toe, and slung him behind bars. "You're going to tell us everything you know, did you hear that kid?" they told him the next day. The torment had begun for the poor boy, interrogations, beatings, on one day yes, and the next as well. "You're going to give in, you little jerk, you'll see how well you're going to sing." Ariel had dreamed he was a hero, but they hadn't told him that the road to the finish line was long and rocky and that not everyone arrived; he closed his eyes tightly, clenched his fists, bit his lips, and didn't give anything away. "You think you're a little tough guy, eh, asshole? You'll end up giving in, you'll see, even the most weather-beaten leather softens up with time. We have plenty of time, that's how it is, you'll see."

It didn't look like he was going to give in, so they changed tactics. "Tomorrow your mom's coming to visit you, she's going to tell you to behave yourself, to be obedient, and you're going to say 'yes' and you're going to be good, do as she wishes, right? You'd better do so, you piece of shit." No sooner said than done. The next day they took him to a room where, indeed, he saw his mom. They were not allowed to hug or display any affection, that was not the visit's purpose. Behind his mom stood a huge police officer, legs spread, hands on her back, his face smeared with a creepy smile. "Speak up Ma'am. Tell your baby—Ariel was an only child—what he has to do so he doesn't have to see with his own eyes what whores like you are for."

There was once a woman who gave birth to seven sons and raised them to be as tough as ebony, compact and in one piece, steadfast in the face of fire, wind, and iron. Any ax that tried to break their spirit would break before they did, and she saw them die one by one because she preferred them dead rather than give in to the caprice of tyranny. The seven Maccabee sons and their mother are difficult models to imitate. No one should be shocked if other mothers and sons succumb, subjected to the same or a similar threat.

Ariel closed his eyes on seeing the orangutan police officer slapping his mother's shoulders. "Open them, fag, look, look closely," he's a sadist, "she likes to be slapped around first, it excites the little whore, and she loves to be undressed, oh, what soft skin, what lovely tits, oh, the forest in which the slut hides her treasures, open your eyes wider, fag, more, like that . . " And Ariel succumbed. Who wouldn't?

Heard from the lips of someone who had experienced that, the story was more than just shocking and heartbreaking. However, now that I know what followed, it cannot have been what Ariel Lima told me. I have some doubt and ask myself to what degree the personality of the immature young man cracked on being subjected to pressures greater than was his capacity for resistance. Thereafter, he changed and began to hallucinate and perceive something other than reality. I'm referring to the fact that, in his version, Ariel told me, the confession he gave regarded the address where Carbó Serviá, Fructuoso Rodríguez, José Machado, and Joe Westbrook were hiding on April 20, 1957. They were survivors of the assault on the Presidential Palace on March 13, an act in which José Antonio Echeverría ("Manzanita"), the head of the civil resistance in Havana, was killed fighting openly against the Batista regime. (Until the morning of the attack, Echeverría and Serviá had been hiding in the San Francisco monastery, at Aguiar and Teniente Rey Streets, where I was living). I have verified that Ariel's confession was incorrect, that he could not have known that address. Why did he lie to me? Did he perhaps need, in his subconscious, to replace the void in him created by his weakness with information about a significant incident, one very important in the revolutionary calendar?

For whatever reason, he gave in, he informed on his revolutionary companions, and became automatically responsible for their disappearance and death at the hands of the henchmen of Colonel Ventura, a Havana police chief of some ill repute. Having taken this step, the stigma of traitor, imposed by his own conscience more than by remorse over his old comrades, seemingly never left him during the remainder of his life—the twenty months in which he had to hide and then work like a slave in the kitchen of a military barracks until the triumph of the revolution and then in La Cabaña prison. It makes me extremely sad to unravel the list of causes and effects in all this mess due to the not just significant but rather decisive role played therein by torture, and how it can drive someone crazy.

He was brought to trial. Prosecutor De la Fuente wanted to eat him alive; he emptied the dictionary of all the harsh, spiteful, callous, cutting, and hurtful words he could find, calling for the death penalty, just one, albeit for him twenty or fifty would have seemed fitting. If he could have asked for that many, he would have. The defense lawyer was carried along by the whirlwind of passions raised by the prosecutor; "he was intimidated, a boy, immature, lacking in responsibility," he repeated and focused on the same thing over and over again, like the blades of a windmill creaking because the shaft needed to be oiled. Ariel Lima was condemned to die by firing squad.

He was held for a week in the gallery of death. He barely spoke a word. He remained alienated, an empty shell, lost in his own stare, as if he were unaware of everything that had happened to him. The other prisoners looked on him as so young, so abandoned, so in need of affection, so screwed up in such a short life, and pitied him. I promised him I would go and see Che and intervene on his behalf.

I did it at the first opportunity. Che replied that it wasn't his call. Rather it was the Court of Appeals that decided; he asked me why the sentence should be annulled? For two reasons, I told him, the first out of common humanity. Probably, Ernesto Guevara, just like Javier Arzuaga, if subjected to the same test, to the same emotional pressure, when they were sixteen, would have succumbed as had Ariel Lima. Secondly, it was politically shrewd, given that the day after the boy's execution, the press in the United States, in Latin America, and in Europe would shout about how the Cuban Revolution lacked any feeling, and how its justice did not distinguish between adults and minors. How it executed both, which would be of little benefit to the revolutionary cause. Useless. I think by then Che had eradicated any feeling from his soul; the more compassion you asked of him, the more he responded with cruelty. Ariel's fate would be decided by the review.

The commandant saw me in the courtroom, like other nights, and I don't know if he interpreted my presence as just more of the same and this hardened his resolve. It's possible. The hearing lasted barely a half hour. The sentence was ratified and an order given to execute Ariel that very night. He saw me again at the door, as he was leaving the courtroom with the people who had been involved in the trial and the guards. As they went out to the street, he raised his hand to me in greeting. He walked in quick strides toward command headquarters. A woman ran in front of them and fell to her knees before the commandant. Everyone stopped to see what he was going to do. "It's Ariel's mom," someone said. I approached. Che walked around her and once on the other side, said: "Madam, I advise you to speak to Father Javier, who they say is a master at consoling and raising people's spirits." And, turning to me, half bossing and half joking: "She's all yours." I helped her to her feet and advised: "Go home now, try and get over the tragedy, and to live without your son, give yourself to God, I will also entrust you to him." I never saw her again. That night I hated Che.

Ariel went before the firing squad. He didn't know that his mother was nearby. I would even hazard a guess that she was not entirely clear about what they were going to do with him; she didn't know they were executing him. Ariel was a pale imitation of his own self.

I believe in the communion of saints,
I believe in the forgiveness of sins,
I believe in the resurrection of the flesh,
and I believe in the everlasting life.
I believe . . . ?
I believe . . . ?
I believe . . . ?
I know that believing is not understanding or
knowing.
Or that it is knowing from the soul.
Believing is flying, being suspended,
in the skies of mystery.
Accepting mystery, submerging oneself in it,
embracing it, giving oneself in to it.
We speak about the mystery of death.
There is no such thing.
Death is alive, one can see.
Even it is the experience
of that which does not return,
that does not count

because it always travels in the third person.
One believes or one does not believe in what
follows,
what comes afterward.
After death?
Mystery,
God,
a compendium of all the mysteries.
Stumbling along in the dark.
I cannot see.
When day breaks
and the light lands in my eyes,
I ask it to enter me
into the soul
and the seeding
of faith.

# 13

I said above that everyone took confession and communion except one of them. That was the one prisoner, however, who was most given to thinking, the most elegant, and the most courteous of all the ones I met in La Cabaña. The penal population there itself thought him the best read and educated of all of them, a polyglot with five languages to his credit, a living dossier on the dense network of international communism, more of an expert than anyone else on political ideologies and currents in Cuba and Latin America. The most radical revolutionaries, influenced by the old windbags of the Communist Party, attributed him with engineering the disappearance of some of their cherished colleagues. Not that he had participated in their death, but rather that he exposed them publicly, on a list of those who, according to his anti-Marxist criteria, hindered the democratic work of the country and had to be silenced. I'm referring to Lieutenant Colonel José Castaño, head of the politico-military Bureau of Intelligence during the time of the dictator Batista.

I valued a lot the journeys on which he took me along the routes of Latin American Communism, its rhythm of expansion, its possibilities, and its limitations. I learned, well, everyone knew. Fifty years later, well-traveled from so many shoes worn down by plains and mountains, more mountains than plains, at the edges or along the spine of the Andes, I can say that many of his words were prophetic as regards the violence with which sister nations of Central and South America fought over power or for one of the ideological formulas of social and political life. I have seen the all too typical and typically blind dictatorships or democracies, so beautiful in theory but half complete in reality, or the radical pro-Communist socialisms like those today that promise and promise, yet we do not know what they will deliver—perhaps like that in Cuba, pyrotechnics. From him I learned about the existence of one Mariátegui, a very Basque last name, within the initial stages of Peruvian Communism. And other facts that were of benefit to me in my next ten years as a missionary. It came as no surprise, then, that some people wanted him to be their friend and others abhorred him and declared him an enemy, on the list of "those to be eliminated."

One day I suggested that he should meet a priest, a friend of mine and teacher of philosophy.

They chatted, exchanged thoughts and opinions, regretted not having met before, yet carried on in their own directions with their daily grind. That was not the best moment to spend time on thinking about ideas.

Castaño's trial devolved into a strange affair. Before him paraded, in their capacity as witnesses for the prosecution, all the main leaders of the Communist Party, Carlos Rafael Rodríguez, Aníbal Escalante, Antonio Núñez Jiménez, Peñalver, Miguel Sampedro, and Alicia Agramonte, all of them attempting to connect the accused to bloody actions. I'm not sure, but the name of Raúl Castro also springs to mind, as if he also wanted to do his bit as a witness to put Castaño in front of a firing squad. The prosecutor Pelayo did not find a means to argue for the death penalty. Trying to establish a connection between reports on the activities of a person and his political ideas, on the one hand, and his disappearance and death, on the other, is not easy, at least when the aim of the findings is not predetermined to eliminate that person. And yet Castaño was sentenced to death. The court, incidentally, was presided over by Commander Víctor Bordón Machado, assisted by six others, all of them officials in the rebel army.

In the opinion of the defense lawyer, the judgment was not conclusive and this led to the suggestion of a hopeful appeal hearing. He wanted to know my reaction to his defense plan. He thought it was fantastic; I thought it was sheer fantasy. It was based on the offer of some kind of exchange. By all accounts, some approaches had been made to the United States ambassador in Cuba; he had already been sounded out on the issue. How about Cuba letting José Castaño move north ehile the United States handed over to Cuba two of the most detested figures of the Batista dictatorship, Ventura and Carratalá? My opinion? I was no expert in international politics or diplomatic agreements, let alone in the law, but I sensed not. Che wouldn't go for that, that such an idea could even be counterproductive given how unpopular the US was: "Do whatever you wish, but in my opinion—no." He looked like someone who'd just seen a box of eggs fall from a moving helicopter without any parachute, like everything had just been smashed to pieces.

Had Ventura and Carratalá ever been returned to Cuba, there would have been a huge street party in Havana, as big as that which greeted Fidel's arrival in January. They would have been paraded like captured animals, in a cage on a moving truck. Or they would have reproduced Francisco Goya's famous painting of the May executions in some public square for everyone to see. But the parties were over some time ago for Che. So that, in the hearing he presided over, the sentence was ratified: José Castaño should be executed, and that very night.

I was heading toward the prison to inform him of the decision and to discuss what we would do in the final two hours of his life. But then Captain Duque Estrada caught up with me and went straight to the point. "You have to come with me, right now, without wasting any time, we're going to see Fidel Castro, we're going to ask him to postpone the execution and review the case again." I couldn't believe what I was hearing. Was this Duque Estrada speaking to me? What was going on? What kind of strange, really strange, turn of events, a full ninety degrees, was this? Incredible. "Wait a moment," I asked him, "I'm going to tell Castaño what's happening, I'll come right back."

Just the two of us. In his jeep. Barely speaking. Through the streets of Havana bathed in darkness. With a knot of hope stirring in my soul. In a race against death. To a meeting with the new owner of lives and worldly goods and properties and fortune in Cuba. Do you give me permission, Fidel my master, to continue living?

At that moment, Fidel was at the headquarters of the sugar union, in its great amphitheater overflowing with people and applause, giving one of his interminable speeches. It was just him on the stage—surrounded by his own light and caressed by his own voice. Full of Fidel, of himself, of his own divinity, as divine as the Roman emperors, as the gods of Olympus, messiah and savior, the revolutionary fantasy in word and flesh.

We got as close as we could to him, in the wings, so that during one of his pauses to stop for breath and absorb the applause, he could see us. He did so and Duque Estrada raised his arms. When he signaled to come to him, we rushed forward. Duque Estrada explained why we were there. "All right, all right, that's fine." He gestured to us that we could go. We went. And? Well, I don't know, I have no idea what "it's fine" meant coming from Fidel in the middle of one of his boring speeches. Perhaps in the absence of Camilo to ask him "am I doing ok?" Fidel was just telling himself "I'm doing fine, I'm doing fine." "'It's fine' could be understood as 'agreed', right Father?" "We're going to make the sign of the Cross and we're going to sleep."

I'd left the car at La Cabaña, so went for it and to tell Castaño what had happened and wish him a good night's sleep. "Fidel said: 'It's fine.'," that is, he's allowing you to live for I don't know how much longer." I was happy because the sun would rise once again and would shine down on us one more time. I left well after one in the morning to go back to the San Francisco monastery and to bed. I was awakened by the tooting of horns and shouts at around three. Everyone on Aguiar Street, between Teniente Rey and Amargura, was leaning out of their windows or balconies, curious to see what all the racket was about. The jeep that was waiting for me with its engine running at the door of the monastery shot off like a rocket as soon as

I set foot inside it. "But what's happened? Fidel told us . . " "Fidel asked us what we were looking for, when he ended his speech, I was contacted by phone, I explained the situation. He asked what Che had decided, I told him and he didn't want to hear any more. So Castaño's going to be executed right now, what are they waiting for?" "But he said before . . " "Forget it, Father, before he didn't even realize what I was speaking to him about." "Fella, this is enough to drive you crazy." "You bet . . "

They had been waiting for us for about an hour at the wall. Not even in those circumstances did they dare proceed without my presence. The six riflemen and a small group of officials were chatting away in the middle of the small square. At the foot of the wall, alone, hands uncuffed, walking round in circles, around and around, around and around, the condemned man. What was he thinking? How would I explain what had happened? What was I going to say? He stopped when he saw me. I went up to him. There was no sign of antipathy or discomfort in his face, absolute serenity. I initiated an apology. "I'm so sorry, forgive me . . " "Forget all that," he interrupted. "I'm not interested," in a full voice, tone unchanged, "it's normal, I expected it, I know them, see, Father, I know them."

Attendance at no other execution was as easy as this one, yet none either, in a certain sense, was as dramatic and painful. "Where do they execute people? Over there by the post? Well, let's walk over there, I want this to be quick, there's very little time to say much more." We walked over. They stopped us six feet from the post. The firing squad took its place. "Father, I'm going to ask you a big favor, I know I have no right to do so, you'll have to see if you want to do it for me . . . I'm going to die . . . you know what I think . . . Father . . . could you, please, lend me your faith so that I may show up with it where I'm going?" I was stunned. It was the last thing I would have thought or expected. I didn't know what to think, I wasn't thinking anything. I hugged him and closed my eyes; I didn't want him to see me crying. I couldn't find any words; I couldn't speak. "My faith? . . . What faith?" I said to myself. I couldn't believe what I was experiencing. "Yes, José, take it, it's yours, take it with you . . " "Thanks Father, I'll die peacefully." We didn't move an inch as we hugged one another, silently, there was nothing else to say. "Say a prayer, Father, so that I might pray with you." We said the Lord's Prayer. Very slowly, pausing after every line, without letting go of one another, " . . . and deliver us from evil. Amen." I held the cross up to his lips. He kissed it. He died with his eyes open, wide open, almost as if they wanted to pop out, run away, as if they were in a hurry to leap into the eternal adventure.

The months of February, March, and April were the toughest. In May—I don't know the reason—there were fewer executions. Perhaps it was

Che's failing health—he was suffering a relapse of chronic asthma and as a consequence was in the throes of a rest and recuperation break at the beach in Tarará—had something to with it. An anonymous voice had let it be known that it was just a rest, that there should not be any speculation, that revolutionary justice did not sleep, and that there was still a huge outstanding account to be settled. The work of the courts was reduced to a snail's pace. By mid-month, the firing squad ceased to let out its midnight roars. In the "gallery of death" the slow drip of those that left never to return dried up and that fact alone reminded the approximately fifteen condemned men that May meant spring. That made them smile as they looked out of the windows of the gallery. We continued to say the rosary every night. They continued to receive communion every morning.

"Make the most of the lull and go and see the doctor," half a warning, half a request, my most cherished voice in Casa Blanca asked me to take care of myself. And I paid heed. I went to see Doctor Ramón Casas. Digging around, amid a pile of questions, in the kin and under the skin, before he'd even spoken a word the doctor's demeanor revealed he was seeing something he didn't like. "Let's see what the lab tests say, but I'm warning you to take care of yourself, and it would be a good idea to take a long vacation." "But what's wrong?" "There's nothing obviously wrong, in the sense of something bad, but it's not all good either, in the sense of being well. You need to rest, let's start there." He spoke with my superior and told him I should stay away from La Cabaña for a good long while. A friend, someone who was preaching at the time in Mexico, was passing through Havana and suggested I leave with him. "On one condition, that it's not to go and work with you, because you're a real workaholic." "Of course, you're coming to rest."

It was decided that I'd travel to Mexico in mid-June. Beforehand, I wanted to visit Commander Guevara at his retreat in Tarará. I must have arranged the visit. The afternoon I showed up, accompanied by Father Mariano Errasti. For the moment, Che was resting, I was told, and then he was going to a very important meeting. I'd have to come back another day. One of those days I made arrangements for a photographer from the magazine *La Quincena* to do a tour of La Cabaña. The report was written by Father Mariano. The photographer was free to work without any pressure, any restrictions, to take whatever photos he wanted for the magazine, and others for his own personal collection.

On June 12, mid-morning, I got on the plane that would take me to the land of Our Lady of Guadalupe, of Archbishop Zumárraga, and of Pancho Villa. I took with me a letter from Dr. Casas addressed to a neurologist friend of his. In Rancho

Boyeros Airport I found out that a few hours later Che Guevara would take another plane heading for the Middle East. I fell asleep and dreamed that the Basque and the Mexican and the Cuban and the Argentinian were waiting for me to take me to meet Moctezuma.

Mexico and my new friends, Basques, Mexicans, an Asturian, and an Aragonese, treated me like a king. They took me all over the place, to Puebla, to Fortín de las Flores, to Teotihuacán, to Cuernavaca, to Querétaro, to Guadalajara, to eat real Mexican snacks, to the movies, to the theater, to eat Basque and Spanish food, to sports events, and even to a bullfight—which I'd never imagined I'd ever see—and then to eat again. "But holy cow! I think I'm going to burst." "Whenever you don't feel like any more, we'll get you ready to go back to Cuba." I was living at the home of a Basque family, arrivals from Sopuerta and from Galdames—the husband pro-Franco, the wife non-committal, an older nephew who was a separatist Basque nationalist with an acerbic side. "And you?" "Me?" I said, "why don't we speak about something else? Yes, anything so long as it's not politics." And it was better that way for me. I had to preach twice in three months, for the Franciscans in the Centenary Park in Coyoacán and in an enchanting snow-capped half-cave church in Amecameca. The sermon was free, but I was presented with a bag of apples that the lady of my house transformed into a lovely exquisite quince.

I only went to see the neurologist three times—on arrival, a month later, and then two months in. A person with a very affable manner, he read the letter by Dr. Casas, plied me with questions. When he had built up a complete picture, he told me about a new medication, still in the experimental stage, which it was hoped would prevent depressive neuroses by blocking out their causes. It was a bit like removing the problem at its roots, and he asked for permission to use it on me. What did I know about such things? I trusted people who I thought were nice and had good intentions, I believed in the expertise and honesty of the physician, and it never occurred to me to ask for a second opinion, putting myself in his hands without any further ado. That's how the chaplain of La Cabaña became a guinea pig. The treatment was very easy to follow: take some pills, eat well, sleep as much as my body wanted, entertain myself, go for walks. I had never followed any other treatment so faithfully. I went for a check-up twice and, on the second occasion, I was given the all-clear. "And how much do I owe you, doctor?" "Nothing, really, you don't owe me a thing, rather it's me who . . " And the guinea pig began to skip around again in its field, confident and happy.

On my return to Cuba, I felt as good as new.

So new, in fact, that I recognized everyone who was living under the same roof, all my work colleagues, all of those who had more or less been close to me. I remembered how each of them was, what they did, if they liked to read or whether they were joke tellers, whether they preferred the songs of Rafael or those of Beni Moré, if they worked on the printing press, in the kitchen, or the sacristy. But I didn't recall their names, and there was nothing I could do to remember them—a warning signal.. On the first day I was shocked. I told them about the treatment and shortly after, amid laughter, everything went back to normal. Strange. My memories of La Cabaña had responded to the treatment in a different way. Many names had been erased forever on the blackboard of my memory, but I remembered the names and the steps of my Stations of the Cross that had affected me the most. I didn't want La Cabaña to stop being an intrinsic part of my life. Unlike my priestly ordination or my being sent to the Americas, it had become like what for my body were my eyes, legs, and kidneys. A few days later I asked Father Luis Lizarralde, who had substituted for me in the parish of Casa Blanca during my absence, to accompany me to La Cabaña. After I had left, they told him that they would call him to go up there on execution nights He did not mind going up there again now. He had ministered to about fifteen men during those months, and had been received correctly but coolly.

Che Guevara's absence had resulted in a drastic change of personnel. No one knew me, it wasn't like it was before when I could move around like I owned the place. Every few steps I was asked to identify myself, I wasn't allowed into the gallery of death, although I was able to find out that several of those I'd left behind were still there, at least the group of five. The aunt of one of them was a nun living in Rome and managed to get a very influential long-robed cardinal to take an interest in him, and, in the process, in the case of the five who were still on death row. We could, however, go to the moat of the laurels without anyone bothering us and spend some time there. I wanted to retrace my steps, connect some dots in my memory, redraw the picture of one particular night, of another, bring to the surface names and details in danger of sinking into the depths of the forgetfulness from which they would never return. The post that we never used was still there, the wall riddled with bullet holes, there, floating in silence, the last prayer, the last embrace. I said goodbye to La Cabaña. I would never return. It would accompany me wherever I went. To be sure, I went back to Mexico. It respected what I wanted to remember, and erased the rest, and everything proceeded without any anxiety or fear, in holy peace and tranquility.

Two months later, at the National Catholic Congress, the General Assembly of Catholic Action was held. I was appointed a national advisor to the Male Youth section. I left the parish in Casa Blanca, I left the San Francisco monastery, and went to live in the Catholic university lodgings in the Vedado neighborhood, wrapped in the cellophane of vanity and embarrassed, at the same time, to accept responsibilities for which I didn't feel prepared. The old ghosts of La Cabaña were shaking my faith there in the face of death and here in the face of life. What kind of inspirational flag, which wasn't just made of brightly colored paper and pretty words, could I hoist for young people to embrace as their own? What kind of example to follow could I give them? God forgive me.

Some months went by, and in June 1960, I traveled to Spain because my father was dying and my superior decided that I should be present when the time came. He assured me I could come back. My return was impeded by the Cuban Consulate in Madrid. That trip gave me the opportunity to see and talk one last time with Commander Ernesto Che Guevara de la Serna.

Three hundred dollars once a year was the maximum amount of foreign money a traveler, passport in hand, could ask for in a bank when going abroad. My passport showed that I had taken out this amount eleven months previously, when I traveled to Mexico. I would take, then, the handful of dollars that my friends wanted, or rather that they could give me, and God be with you. I remembered that Che was the great banker of Cuba, the president of the National Bank no less, he who stamped his famous Che as a signature on an issue of new Cuban peso bills. His office was six or seven feet away from the San Francisco monastery, on the other side of Amargura Street.

He received me very attentively and talkatively, like on that Epiphany day in La Cabaña. I explained to him the motive of my visit. The intransigent revolutionary, he of the strict adherence to the law, he of unblemished justice and exemplary punishment, asked me: "And how much would you be disposed to robbing the government of, which is like robbing the people?" "Well to tell the truth, robbing it, bless my soul, Commander, robbing it, not a single *centavo*, requesting from it, the three hundred the law states, and if I were to 'stretch that out', if the government allowed itself to be 'stretched', then a little more." "Have you brought five hundred *pesos*? I'll let you have that much and no more. Give them to me and I'll give you five hundred dollars." "And you won't send me to prison for trying to bribe you?" "It's true that I should? You yourself acknowledge that, but you'll see now how the heart of the revolution beats." He opened one of the draws in the desk, took out a roll of twenty-dollar bills, counted them up to twenty-five and gave them to me. We chatted a while about his health, about my wish to return to Cuba, about how the revolution was progressing. "Well, I like some things and not others, like you I'm sure." I agreed, some things yes and not others. When I got up to shake his hand and say goodbye, he asked me a question that still, today, fifty-one years after his having asked it and forty-four years after his death in the star-crossed adventure in Bolivia, continues to niggle away at me: "How would you categorize the relationship we've had since we first met each other?" I looked at him, not exactly stunned by the question, but certainly very surprised. I would never have imagined him asking it. He awaited the answer with his eyes, like needles, transfixed on mine. I weighed and measured my thoughts. "I would say it has been a friendly relationship of sorts, getting there at least, but I wouldn't dare to say that it crystallized into an authentic friendship." "That's true," he replied, "we haven't been friends, you tried to bring me over to your side and failed; I tried to get you on my side and failed. Whenever we meet again without the masks we're wearing now we'll be enemies, face to face." A shiver went down my spine and from head to toe. I had to answer him, but had no idea what to say. "Masks you say? Commander, I've never worn a mask, I don't know what that is." We continued to gaze at one another for a while. I swear that neither he nor I did so as enemies. We shook hands. "Have a good trip," he said. "Good luck," I replied. And I left the office.

Midday, Sunday.
There is a living silence and it is the sole
owner
of the silence
in the moat of the laurels,
the square of death.
Words have clawed their way up
the walls of the rampart,
they have hidden in the cracks,
next to the moss.
The rampart drips fragrances
of silence.
A gust of wind enters and prowls around
the corners,
like an emaciated and long-tailed dog
half-totting along in search of his master.
It stops at the base of a stick.
It is the pole of death.
"Who are you looking for?"
"My owner."

"Your owner went.
He fell down right there.
And they took him away
in a cheap pine box."
"And how do you know? Who told you?"
"I'm a witness.
A silent witness, a friend of the silence.
I belonged to a chestnut tree.
They cut it down at a bad time."

"An artist took a piece away
and made a Saint Francis out of it
with a dove on his shoulder.
Something else much sadder was my luck.
They brought me here to be the post
with a chain down my back
that waits night and day
for the condemned
who in order to die standing up
needs to have his body strapped to mine.
I gather up his last scream,
I soothe the last beat
of his heart."
"Is that what happened to my boss?"
"No. So far this year
they haven't trussed up anyone.
All have asked to die
Without being blindfolded,
standing on their own two feet."
"And no one has faltered?"

"No one."
"Why?"
"I don't know.
Some speak about hypnosis,
others speak about faith,
I don't know.
Ask the silence, which in this square
Serves as the echo of death."

# 14

It was understood that midnight was the space in time that ran from twelve at night to three in the early morning. It happened very rarely before twelve or after three. I'm referring to the events in La Cabaña during the first five months of 1959. At midnight the revolutionary courts unleashed their hatred and spewed out their sentences: twenty years, thirty years, life, condemned to death. At midnight the gallery of death bled from the agony of each goodbye of those who were going on their way to the firing squad and welcomed in those coming to replace them and to learn how to die. At midnight I regretted not having the gift of bilocation, multiplied by two, in order to be able to be at the same time in the courts, in the gallery of death, and anywhere else I was called to fight the shadows, for God's sake! It was me, at midnight, spreading light and spreading hope, and I barely had any myself. At midnight the caravan of death proceeded unhurried along the narrow cobblestone street, crossed the bridge over the moat, came out onto the esplanade, turned right, greeted the giant cold cement Christ our Lord, and went into the moat of laurels. At midnight a firing squad of six soldiers prepared, rifles raised to shoulders, to cut short the life of a man, or two, or three, all those that were led before them. At midnight one man or two or three, those that had been singled out, standing up and head held high, prepared to die. At midnight I spoke to that man about how God was light, was love, was waiting on the other side of death. I said with him the Lord's Prayer, gave him to kiss the crucifix that I was holding in my hand, hugged him goodbye. At midnight the rifles roared and a body fell to the ground and night became more night. At midnight mystery enveloped us all, a mystery without any answers, where are you Jesús, Pedro, Luis, José? Where are you all? A mystery, the dawn, for believers. At midnight . . .

There were three protagonists of the events in La Cabaña at that time: he who died, he who killed, and I, God's clown, seeking to give what he didn't possess. I was thirty years-old at the time, and, with the fifty-three years that have subsequently passed to this day, January 6, 2012, that makes me eighty-three. Those of us whose life's paths crossed there and could then shake hands and ask ourselves, like two friends after a long trip, "and how was it for you?"

It is useless asking Pedro Morejón and the fifty-four others who followed him – I only know of fifty-four, the only ones during those first five months, the ones I attended to. Not even the antennas of faith could pick up their response. We can believe, but we do not know. If we believe that present life merges at the moment of death into another, like a drop of water in a river merging into the ocean where the river discharges, if that's what we believe, those fifty-five are still alive. And will they be happy? Of course with the happiness we experience here, no. And no one knows what happiness is like in that other life. We believe that they are alive and that they are happy. And will we meet them one day? I'd like to, but I don't know, perhaps. With those that have died there is only contact through memory and faith. I would have liked to stay in touch with their families; for example, with that of Jesús Sosa Blanco. I have a vague idea that someone told me they had moved to Canada, and that one of the daughters took vows in a religious order. A life as I had for ten years, continuously on the go and without any fixed postal address, is not the best grounds for cultivating friendships. Long live everyone, alive and dead, under the shelter of Love.

I said that the second protagonist was he who pulled the trigger and cut short lives. He who obeyed orders. And his superior. On up to the "heads," those who from on high dictated what the revolution was and how it was to be carried out. The "how was it for you?" aimed at those in charge of what happened in La Cabaña would place us across from Fidel Castro and Ernesto "Che" Guevara. The latter is dead already. And peace to the dead. Peace, period. That's how it should be, although . . .

Che Guevara is a myth. That is so whether we like it or not, for good and for bad. I doubt very much whether he would like that. In love with an ideal and faithful to its postulates, he lived and applied them. In the process, he ended up being harsh, very harsh; cruel, very cruel. Did this make him arrogant or did arrogance make him like that? I don't know. He was, though, conceited. And assured, very sure of himself. Above all, he was convinced and with not a screw loose, identified totally with the Marxist-Maoist ideal, no matter who got hurt or how in the process, including death. For me, his first big mistake was reading history—and anthropology and economics and sociology—from someone else's perspective, Karl Marx and company, and transforming what he'd read into dogma. I respect those that may think like that if they respect in turn what the rest of us think, but I think they are wrong. His second big mistake was to believe that the rebels in the Sierra Maestra won a war and that, by repeating the same events in any other setting, they would win and win and win other wars, all wars, that it was just a question of time.

How could men who considered themselves so smart believe such a crazy idea? The fancies of the human mind are truly unpredictable. He fell victim to that stupid belief. What I most admired in him was his sincerity and that he never hid behind anyone for his own protection, as did others in the Sierra and outside of it. I want to state, too, that in the eagerness to demonize Che a lot of lies have been told.

I do not know the authors of such claims, but I have read on the Internet that, on January 2, he ordered and participated in the execution of some forty people, without trial. It is also said that, during his time as commander of La Cabaña, Che ordered (in this case after trials) many executions—according to one accounting, three hundred and fifty victims, and, to another, more than five hundred. He is said to have taken part in the executions. Another claim was that on November 26, 1959, he ordered the execution (with or without trial is unstated) fifty people, also in La Cabaña. None of this is true. Did he kill in the Sierra Maestra, did he kill in Santa Clara, did he kill in the Congo, did he kill in Bolivia? They say he did and that he killed a lot. I don't know. But in La Cabaña, in 1959, he ordered the death penalty for fifty-five men, but he neither personally killed nor was present at the execution of anyone. I hope that, with time, the fervor of those who elevated him to the altars of mythology diminishes and disappears; I do not understand why they did so in the first place, and even less so after knowing him. Whatever the case, I said it above: "peace to the dead."

Che left Cuba over differences with Fidel. As I said once and I'll repeat now, "they were not trees meant for the same forest." He left to redeem the world, convinced that, to do so, he had to gain power through a hail of bullets, in guerrilla warfare. In the process, and I don't know whether spontaneously, a "new man" would emerge. He went first to Africa, to the Congo, where he did not redeem anything or anyone, and then to Bolivia, where he fared no better. They say he told those who were going to kill him that he was more useful alive than dead. I think so, but others didn't, and they exterminated him. That day, seven years after my meeting him for the first time in La Cabaña, the world found out that Che Guevara had died in Bolivia. I was in Lima. That afternoon marked the start of the novena of The Lord of Miracles, and I had been entrusted with saying the corresponding mass. My initial words on that occasion were, more or less, the following: "A man has died!" And, turning to Christ nailed to the cross that looked down on the proceedings from the pulpit, "You know of whom I am speaking, I hope You have shown pity on him, and that You have gone to seek him to lead him to the House of the Father." I have thought on more than one occasion that I would have liked to have been closer to Che when it came time for him to depart. Who knows if he felt the same about me?

Of course I'd like to ask Fidel: "How was it for you?" Even though we know his reply. Good, really good, excellent. The revolution, immaculate since its conception and triumphant to the end. Its enemies, all of you, those that did not want to even listen to or understand me, and especially the United States, that Satrap of the Devil, you are responsible for things not turning out better." Fidel, as we know, was like "a leopard that cannot change its spots." No one understands Fidel, not even he himself.

What can I add to what has been said both for and against the Cuban revolution? In my opinion, Fidel Castro's out-of-control personality meant that, from very early on, the waters of the revolution were likely to overflow and overwhelm, flooding any terrain into which they came into contact and ruining all that they came across there. If he had led it in a more measured fashion, without getting trapped in the net of his own colossal ego, without seeing everyone who was not his lap dog as an enemy, including his closest comrades, if he had known how to listen, if in appearing as a "David" capable of beating the "Goliath" of the North he hadn't given in to the interests and imperatives of the other "Goliath" of the East, if just once he would have acknowledged humbly an error, just one, if he hadn't lied over and over and over, and if he hadn't hated so so so much and if he hadn't listened to himself again and again and again, if he'd shown just a minute fraction of the love for his people that he is said to have shown for himself . . . the revolution could have been a lot better. It might have been so despite the enemies that he had from the beginning and that he still has and who are very powerful. But the thing is that the worst enemy of the revolution was on the inside, deep inside, right at its very heart. It was the neurotic, out-of-control Fidel Castro himself. How can one lose a game while holding all the trump cards and four aces? Whoever knows the answer to that, please tell me.

Fidel Castro is two years older than me: eighty five. How long has he got left? And then? Does anyone think the Cuban revolution has a future without Fidel? Not me. Cuba saddens me, its uncertain future, what Cubans both there and outside Cuba will do, taught, as they both are, to so despise and hate each other.

Now it just remains to recount what happened to me. I'll say first where I've been. In June of 1960, I went to my homeland, the Basque Country, and experienced my father's death and, three days later, that of my oldest brother in a fatal car accident in which we were all injured and he died. I couldn't go back to Cuba because they wouldn't let me in. In 1961, I was assigned to a Missionary

Team in the Americas. I joined it in Medellín, Colombia, and traveled with it throughout the rest of the country, passing through Ecuador. Then I was sent to Miami for a year on a special mission. I then rejoined the Team in El Salvador and we hopped from there to Peru. It was there that I was chosen to be Team leader. I declined, but my superiors insisted, and I told them "you'd better be careful I don't end up the gravedigger rather than the leader." And sure enough, in 1968, I oversaw the burial of the Missionary Team for the Americas.

Throughout this time, I preached as often and as best I could. I came into contact with a lot of bishops and a couple of cardinals. From this contact, I drew the conclusion that in the Church, at the level of the hierarchy, clergymen were the least likely to herald and experience the "Kingdom of God," according to the Gospel of Jesus, and are the most likely to make of the Church a bone dislocated from the path of social progress. It was a church that was out-of-date, backward-looking, and just cruising along. Despite all that, I still loved it because it was my church. I was often weak and lazy and spent a lot of time thinking that the grass was greener on the other side. I wrote something that my superior didn't like. Did I deserve a reprimand and did I need any help? Neither, but quite to the contrary. I don't understand how some men manage to become bishops or high-ranking officials in religious orders. I was expelled. "Go wherever you want, but go far away, get out of my sight." That superior would never again rear his head or crush my dreams as if they were wings.

In 1974 I was a plank washed up by the ocean's waves on a beach in Puerto Rico, the mortal remains of a shipwreck, the residue of disappointment and disillusion. I spoke to three psychologists, two of them priests. They all thought that more harm than good was done in the Church, and they advised me to leave the priesthood. I sent that request to Rome, and they responded faster than firefighters called to a blaze, which prompted one friend to say, "it seems like it was a good idea, and don't even think about going back."

I could now marry. I met a young woman who lived near the beach. She proposed marriage. "But I'm a lot older than you." "It doesn't matter." "It could matter." "I said it didn't matter." And we wed. She rowed, she took the helm, she bailed out the water, and despite the fact that, because of me, we had to navigate heavy seas and upheavals, she led me to shore safe and sound and saved me. We raised three children. Thirty-seven years later, we're not rich, but we are happy.

I have not resolved my crisis of faith. Or rather, I have resolved it, but without looking back. I won't reveal all, nor see the need to do so, but I have renounced all dogmas that I consider to have been fabricated in the workshops of theologians.

I believe in God as the Life that gives birth to all life, the source of creation, love, energy, and light, omnipresent, the essence of everything that exists, and in whom we all become related. And I believe in Jesus and his Gospel, his good news, his "kingdom," his salvation through love, truth, and justice—and "what more do you need?" I ask myself. And I feel the winds of Peace blowing gently within me.

Recently, I was sent a video that a friend filmed in the streets of Havana and in La Cabaña. It was news to me: the La Cabaña I knew and experienced was different. They had pressure-cleaned the stones, they had had the good taste not to paint any of the exterior ones, they had removed all the bars and tons of iron, without doubt, and the only bit they had left was exposed on the new doors simulating the heads of the nails that had pulled out. The prison courtyard is an uncluttered open space, with a stage on which artists must perform, portraying historical characters that lived there. The entrances to the galleries are open, I suppose now dedicated to different chapters in history, part of the museum that has come to form part of the new La Cabaña. The main door to the chapel and the corridor to the gallery of death is closed, and for all my friend's attempts to try and find someone who could and wanted to open it, he was unsuccessful. So it was impossible to see how they have maintained that point at which I used to turn white on the outside while burning up on the inside. The galleries that served as courts are now inviting, painted in a light cream color with their glass display cabinets and shelves, showcases of ancient history perhaps, but not of the history of hatred and pain experienced there scarcely fifty years ago. My friend went over to the "moat of the laurels." A kind of marble plinth with an inscription and surrounded by a chain fence—I assume in honor of some great patriot who was executed on that spot—has been placed where those condemned to death took their turns when there were several of them in line to be executed. And imagine my surprise when I saw the execution wall still intact, with the only change being that the post has been dug up and removed. The rains and the accumulated dirt have darkened the bullet holes in the wall that, fifty years ago, were white. What memories!

I don't think it captures the reality, but I would like to go back to Cuba. And once there, before anything else and more than anything else, I'd like to go up to La Cabaña and through the rite of recollection, and, with neither drumrolls nor spotlights, summon up the angels, spirits, and ghosts that must still hover around there, like seagulls, among the old, dark, worn-out stones.

Fifty-one years later,
everything beats, still alive,
an "alive" softened by the passage of time,
reflected in the screen of memory.
The shadows, the noises, the words,
the gallery, the moat, the wall,
the small square, the voices of death,
the men who killed,
the men who died.
And a Christ,
silent, rigid, cold,
raised in one of my hands.
The same Christ,
this metal one, that cement one,
which I rebuked as if in reproach,
in accompanying the condemned men,
on the way to the firing squad,
at midnight.
"Who are you? What are you doing there?
Why don't you come down and come along
with me?

These men need you.
I also need you."
And Christ didn't speak,
he didn't come down,
he didn't move.

66683411R00129

Made in the USA
Middletown, DE
07 September 2019